Jesus—
Lord for
All Times

DONALD G. DAWE

JOHN KNOX PRESS
ATLANTA, GEORGIA

D1468765

Credit is acknowledged to the following for use of Scripture quotations: Quotations from the *Revised Standard Version of the Bible,* copyrighted 1946 and 1952 by the Division of Christian Education of the National Council of Churches, are used by permission.

From the Today's English Version of the New Testament. Copyright © American Bible Society 1966, 1971.

From the Jerusalem Bible. Copyright © 1966 by Darton, Longman & Todd, Ltd. and Doubleday & Company.

From *The New English Bible.* © The Delegates of the Oxford University Press and the Syndics of The Cambridge University Press, 1961, 1970. Reprinted by permission.

Copyright © 1975 by John Knox Press
All Rights Reserved
Printed in the United States of America

Contents

Introduction

Writing about Jesus today, one is confronted with the dilemma of the writer of the Gospel according to John: there is so much to tell about Jesus! "But there are also many other things which Jesus did; were every one of them to be written, I suppose that the world itself could not contain the books that would be written." (John 21:25)

The Gospel writer was referring simply to the details of the crowded, busy, earthly life of Jesus. We today also know at least part of the continuing story of what the risen Christ has done to those who have faith in him. How is it possible to pick and choose from this rich and complex story what to put into one small book?

Finding What to Say

The Gospel writer had his means of selection readily at hand: "Now Jesus did many other signs in the presence of the disciples, which are not written in this book; but these are written that you may believe that Jesus is the Christ, the Son of God, and that believing you may have life in his name." (John 20:31) Among the variety of means by which we can be introduced to Jesus, John suggests a key one: to find life in him and deepen our fellowship with him, we need to be exposed to Jesus as he lived on earth. That is the basic approach of this book.

Our hope simply is that by rethinking and reliving the ways in which people encountered Jesus in the past, we will deepen and clarify our relationship to him now. Then, as his disciples, we can go on to seek his path through today's world.

To be sure, there are deep and vital differences between the first and the twentieth centuries. But if there is more to life than color TV and indoor plumbing, fast cars and instant foods, we should be able to see our efforts to know and live faithfully with Jesus foreshadowed in people in first century Palestine. After all, we, like them, are struggling to find meaning and hope and joy in the face of emptiness and guilt and death. We, like them, are up against the fact that our lives are rushing to an uncertain end, and we wonder if the rush has any purpose. We, like them, are struggling against injustice, violence, and fear. By taking a deep look at the friends and foes of Jesus in the first century and then at ourselves, we can see how our lives measure up against the reality of Jesus and his truth. We can start to find ourselves and see how we stand before his claims on our lives.

The main features of the story of people's encounters with Jesus emerge from the New Testament. But the New Testament has to be read against its background in the Old Testament. It also comes most fully to life when placed in its historical setting; to better understand his often misguided friends and his implacable foes—the converted, the half-converted, and the unconverted whom we meet in the Gospels—we have to take into account the religious sectarians and political fanatics who made the world of Jesus so much like our own. We shall even take a beginning look at the mysterious religious sect of the Essenes, whose writings were unearthed about thirty years ago in caves by the Dead Sea.

Finding Your Own Way

Any book about Jesus must, by its very nature, have a kind of "do-it-yourself" aspect to it. If the message of this book is to have meaning for you, you have to retrace the story on your own through the Bible itself. To aid in this, the main Biblical references are included in the text. However, don't be satisfied with the interpretation until you have tested it yourself or with a group of friends.

The many new translations will help in your understanding. Through them you can listen in new ways to the vivid, everyday language of Jesus and those around him. Most of the Biblical quotations in this book are from the Revised Standard Version. Whenever other translations are used they are indicated by an abbreviation after the reference.

NEB indicates *The New English Bible* (Oxford University Press and Cambridge University Press, 1970). This translation brings some striking new insights to the understanding of the Bible. Done by scholars of the churches in England and Scotland, it often reflects British usage of English.

TEV is *The New Testament in Today's English Version* (American Bible Society, 1966). This translation is best known in its paperback edition, *Good News for Modern Man*. It is a fresh translation from the original into modern American usage.

JB is *The Jerusalem Bible* (Doubleday and Co., 1966). This is a one volume translation and commentary for laymen prepared by a group of Roman Catholic scholars. It gets its name from the school of Biblical studies in Jerusalem in which it was written.

Occasionally reference is made to K.J.V., the famous King James Version of 1611 in order to show how much of our traditional religious language has been shaped by this great translation.

There are other editions of the Bible that you may find helpful also. We do need to remember one point about modern versions of the Bible. There is a vast difference between a new translation made directly from the Hebrew text of the Old Testament and the Greek text of the New and the many paraphrases and so-called expanded versions. A paraphrase or amplified version is really a kind of commentary. It gives you the words of Scripture as read out of the theological vision of its writer. As such, these versions do not have the authority of a translation made directly from the original languages. We have used in this book only translations. These provide the reader a chance to build and test his own convictions about Jesus from as direct a contact with the sources as possible.

A great historian once said that you never understand the past until there has been "a fusion of horizons" between your field of vision and those of the people of the past. To know Jesus truly we have to become aware of those places where our lives touch his and where our vision is like that of the people who surrounded him. But when we think about Jesus, we are not dealing simply with someone who is locked in the past and whom we must strain to see. Rather, in a wonderful way he is ever coming forward to meet us in our own time and place. It is this strange power and presence of

Jesus that makes it possible to know him now as we can never know a Thomas Jefferson or a Harriet Tubman.

The final aim of every evangelical book about Jesus—from the child's story book to the most subtle book of theology—is to bring us to new life in him. We need to know the facts about Jesus and those who gathered about him, both friend and foe. We need to know how these men and women reacted to him and why. But these facts must never become simply bits of interesting information from the past. Instead, they become important as the means for pointing us to him. To recall these stories is to call each of us to answer a very personal question: "What importance does Jesus have for me?"

HEAD OF CHRIST

Georges Rouault (1871-1958)

The Cleveland Museum of Art, gift of Hanna Fund.

In this painting a modern artist reflects on the humanity of Christ.
How does this picture relate Jesus to our present-day situation?

CHRIST BETWEEN HIS PARENTS, RETURNING
FROM THE TEMPLE
Rembrandt (1606-1669)

The Metropolitan Museum of Art, Bequest of Mrs. H. O. Havemeyer, 1929.
The H. O. Havemeyer Collection.

Here a great artist concentrates on showing the humility, even ordinariness of Jesus. Neither he nor his parents are pictured as great heroic figures. What aspect of Christian faith in Jesus does this picture reflect? How does this painting help us in relating to Jesus?

CHRIST HEALING THE BLIND MAN

Block print by Robert O. Hodgell

A modern artist depicts a dramatic incident in the life of a man
touched by Jesus. What does this picture convey about the meaning
of our relationship with Jesus?

THE SERMON ON THE MOUNT
Fred Nagler
Courtesy Midtown Galleries, New York City

This modern artist portrays Jesus in a teaching relationship with others. How does this picture present the authority of Jesus?

THE LORD OUR JUDGE

French artist, c. 1250

Bodleian Library, Oxford, England. From a color filmstrip taken from mediaeval religious pictures. Photo by John C. Goodwin.

This picture is from an illustrated Bible prepared for moral instruction. What aspect of Christian faith about Jesus does this drawing express? What element of the Biblical picture of Jesus does this picture tend to neglect?

THE SMALL CRUCIFIXION

Mathis Grünewald (c. 1465-1528)

National Gallery of Art, Washington, D.C.,
Samuel H. Kress Collection, Loan.

This great artist has painted a scene showing the agony of the crucifixion. How is this agony reflected in each figure in this scene?

1 | Jesus and the "Old Time Religion"

Modern people have often concluded that they are finished and done with Jesus. "What," it is asked, "could a first century Jew have to do with our twentieth century world of space travel and nuclear bombs, of rebellious youth and angry parents, of pollution and street crime? Surely Jesus of Nazareth has slipped quietly over the horizon into the oblivion of forgotten history."

Yet Jesus lives on. And he lives on not only in our church school classes and in revivalist preaching; in the preaching, praying, and singing of thousands of churches; in the wall plaques and family Bibles of millions of homes; or in the B.C. and A.D. of our calendars. The great new fact of our time is that Jesus is back in a thousand different ways in our towns and on our campuses.

Jesus is back in our midst in thousands of pop art posters, paperback books, and bumper stickers. There is Jesus the Superstar of the pop records. There is the revolutionary image of Jesus enshrined by the angry poor of the world, for whom he is not just a means of heavenly escape but the hope for a this-world liberation. In contrast there is Jesus the answer, the personal consoler who makes people happy and solves all their personal problems. There is the mystical Jesus, pictured as the Guru to the spaced-out generation. In strange ways, he is being sought by the young people who were raised on materialism and now want mysticism. There is the Jesus of the street Christians who praise him with guitars while wearing tie-dyed jeans and rumpled shirts. There is the Jesus of the establishment people, who extoll him as the source of law and order, and praise him with robed choirs and thunderous organs. There are claims being made for a Black Christ by those who see in the pale Jesus of religious art only a poor reflection of the Savior they know and worship. Some would make claims for a Jewish Jesus. Christians, it is said, have obscured with their theology the real Jesus who was born as a Jew and lived as a Jew.

The arguments among those holding these views about Jesus are often sharp and tense. The more radical claims offend long standing convictions and deeply rooted pieties. Yet these very claims are stirring the interest and shaping the faith of thousands of people today. Doubtless you yourself could add to this list of claims made about Jesus. But, more importantly, you may be examining your own faith in him, for, amid this babel of claims and counter-claims, many are left wondering, sometimes wistfully, sometimes angrily, about how to find the truth.

One thing is certain. Jesus remains very much a part of the unfinished business of men and women in every age. Jesus is God's question to the world. We are all caught up in some way or another in making decisions about him. Even when we throw up our hands in despair, or settle for pictures of him as a "great religious teacher," we have, wittingly or unwittingly, made our own picture of him. Every fragmentary and imperfect picture we form of him represents our attempt to find out who he really is.

Who Is the Real Jesus?

The question is an old one that stands at the heart of the Christian story. Even the dilemma of many answers is as ancient as the question itself. Strangely enough, we hear the question first from the lips of Jesus. He asked his disciples, "Who do men say that I am?" (Mark 8:27) He was ranked, they responded, among the highest and the best. Some said he was Elijah. Who could ask for more? Elijah was the prophet translated by God to heaven in a fiery chariot. Pious Jews fervently believed that with his return to earth, God would bring in the kingdom (Mal. 4:5). Others saw in Jesus the return of John the Baptist, that great teacher of righteousness whose mouth was only stilled by a cruel execution. Others ranked him with Jeremiah or one of the prophets.

On other occasions, Nicodemus acknowledged him as a rabbi, a teacher sent from God, while he was hailed as a Son of David, a member of the royalty established by God, by the crowds. But never once did Jesus stop to acknowledge these high honors or to thank his followers for their admiration.

On the other hand his opponents called him a deceiver. His family at times feared he was mad. He was hailed before the religious court, the Sanhedrin, as a blasphemer. He was brought before a Roman court as a subversive. But with his opponents, as with his followers, Jesus refused to deal in slogans. He felt no more need to refute his opponents than to correct his disciples in their search for a name for him. Rather, he pushed each one of them into facing the question of his true identity in very personal terms: "But who do you say that I am?"

Slogans are finally not enough, when up against the basic questions of life. Shouting our favorite slogans about Jesus at one another creates only noise, not truth. In finding the real Jesus, the important thing is not our slogans about him but our own relationship to him. When questioned about the authority of his teachings, Jesus did not repeat a creed but asked for a response of obedience and faith: "My teaching is not mine, but his who sent me; if any man's will is to do his will, he shall know whether the teaching is from God or whether I am speaking on my own authority." (John 7:16-17) The truth about Jesus is found when you stand in some kind of a relationship with him. So the search for the real Jesus inevitably becomes personal. Someone else's answer may be your guide or help, but in the end it is not enough.

The struggle in every age to know the truth about Jesus is a clash between the people who want to claim him for themselves and those who accept his claim on them. People who would not admit rejecting Jesus have twisted and distorted him so they could claim him for their own way of life. According to the New Testament, whether such people were complimenting him or cursing him, Jesus stood in silent majesty refusing to play their word games. But to those who accepted his claim on their lives and became disciples, he granted the gift of life. When in faith we stop trying to put Jesus into our scheme of things and let him put us into his scheme of things, we will find the real Jesus.

Our present-day search for the real Jesus can be guided and

shaped by the struggle to know him authentically that took place in first century Palestine. By searching the Gospels, the tracts of the Jewish rabbis, the journals of Roman historians, and those strange and fascinating scrolls found some years ago by the Dead Sea, the outlines of an intense drama start to emerge. Bit by bit from the pages of history the story emerges. It was the struggle of four groups of people in ancient Palestine who tried to find the true measure of Jesus.

1) The Pharisees, Sadducees, and priests presided over the religious and political establishment of their day.

2) The Zealots were religious revolutionaries. They wanted to free their people from Roman oppression and establish the kingdom of God in a frenzy of violence.

3) Most of the Essenes lived in a monastery at Qumran by the Dead Sea. They had withdrawn to engage in mystic study and contemplation and to await the coming of the end of the world.

4) Finally there were the disciples, who came to confess Jesus as Lord and who found life transformed in him.

Each one of these groups claimed they had the real measure and meaning of Jesus. They all, in their own way, had made their decisions about him. And whether they realized it or not, these were life and death decisions that shaped their personal destinies.

However, the story of these groups and their search for the truth about Jesus is not simply the story of "Once upon a time, in a faraway land. . . ." The story of their struggles to know Jesus is in a very real sense our story as well. The names may have changed, but their life styles have lived on in our midst to this day. Perhaps you will be able to see your own quest for a deeper insight into and faith in Jesus foreshadowed in their stories.

The Religion of the Establishment

It is difficult to present a fair picture of the men who presided over the religious and political establishment of Jesus' day. Like all who have power, the Pharisees, Sadducees, and priests often used their power with too little concern for the poor and oppressed. Yet any student of New Testament times realizes that these groups have been treated badly by Christian tradition.

The Pharisees have come in for the most unjust condemnation.

The very word "Pharisee" has become a synonym in modern English for a self-righteous, arrogant person. Despite the fact that Pharisees like Nicodemus and Paul became disciples of Jesus, Jesus' conflict with some Pharisees has blinded many Christians to the greatness of the Pharisaic tradition. It is too easy to fall into a kind of inverted snobbery when reading the story of the Pharisee and tax collector going up to the Temple to pray (Luke 18:9-14). We are all tempted to say, "Thank God I am not like that Pharisee." But if we can resist the temptation to become proud about our supposed humility, we can start to grasp the real grounds for the struggle between Jesus and the Pharisees.

To the Pharisees and their priestly associates at the time of Jesus fell the task of maintaining the religious and political establishment of their day. The task was one of almost overwhelming difficulty. On the one hand, they were struggling to preserve what little measure of political and religious freedom they had under the crushing power of the Roman conqueror. On the other hand, they had to keep quiet and obedient a restless people who had produced and welcomed a succession of false messiahs, rabble rousers, and revolutionaries. They had to walk a kind of tightrope between anarchy and despotism.

These religious leaders were part of a great tradition with a noble history. The Pharisees, for example, trace their origins to the sixth century B.C., when the Jews were in exile in Babylon. They struggled to keep their faith alive. As the very name Pharisee implies, these men were "the separated ones," "the seceders," who wanted to keep themselves unstained by the ideas and practices of a pagan world.

They were as a result zealous patriots. In the struggle against Persian, Greek, and Roman oppression, many of the Pharisaic party were numbered among the martyrs and the saints. Less than a century before Jesus' time, eight hundred of them were crucified in Jerusalem by Alexander Jannaeus for rebuking his arrogance and immorality.

So let us never misjudge the Pharisees. They wanted much that most of us want in our time. To put it in modern terms, they wanted safe streets, pious homes, and the Bible in the schools. Furthermore, their plans were informed by a kind of hardhearted political realism. They were not simply pious and irrelevant. To support their cause they would do business even with a Herod or a Pilate. The modern folk theologian, Clarence Jordan, was very near the mark when, in his contemporary translation of the Gospels, he paraphrased the word "Pharisee" as "church member," "priest" as "minister," and "high priest" as "denominational executive."

These men were deeply involved, even as we probably are, in trying to preserve some freedom for their religion, some order in their nation, and some morality for their youth. When we look at these religious leaders who opposed Jesus, we are not looking at unbelievers or idolaters, nor at immoral or unpatriotic people. Instead, we are looking at people that are strikingly like us. While at times they may have degenerated to pettiness and legalism, they did so in pursuit of high ideals. Zeal in defense of God and right seemed no fault to them, no matter how harshly they were judged by the outsiders who were working to undermine the faith they held and the freedom they had. God had spoken, they said, and they were called to preserve this truth. If they were willing to call out the police or National Guard to put down riots, it was because great issues were at stake.

Danger or Deliverance?

As these Pharisees, Sadducees, and priests looked at Jesus, they saw not salvation but danger. At first with tentative questions, then with hostile invective and veiled warnings, and finally with murderous plot, they conspired to rid themselves and their people of this threat.

Jesus' teaching, they believed, undid the very possibility of public morals with his radical ethic of inward conversion and love. When he taught "You, therefore, must be perfect, as your heavenly Father is perfect," he cut the basis from under all the little pat "do's and don'ts" that too easily are treated as the heart of one's moral duty. His talk of a kingdom of God that was coming threatened to unsettle the nicely balanced political arrangements they had reached with the Romans.

Jesus' character also threatened them. His boldness made their uneasy truce with their oppressors more uneasy still. When a restless and despairing people rallied in hope and joy around him, they saw

only the beginnings of civic chaos. When disciples sensed in Jesus
the very presence of God himself, the Pharisees could hear only
blasphemy against the exalted God they worshiped. When those
strange reports of healings came to their ears, they could think only
of trickery, magic, or even demonic works.

When Jesus was at last crucified, they wanted him to be out of
the way forever. A final precaution was taken. A guard was set at
his tomb, lest the disciples come and steal the body away. Jesus, they
argued before Pilate, was an impostor. If his resurrection could be
faked, "the last fraud will be worse than the first." (Matt. 27:64)

Their sincere concern was to protect their people from a cruel
hoax. They believed the disciples were impostors anxious to escape
the drudgery of their fisherman's life for the honor and ease of sitting
at the right hand of a Messiah-Savior. Having done away with a
blasphemer, they were not to become the victims of some impostors.
A gullible and ignorant people had to be protected. The truth of God
and the civil order had to be preserved at all costs.

Such a reading of the Gospels from the perspective of the
Pharisees, Sadducees, and priests seems to us like reading through
a distorting mirror. Facts about Jesus are there, but the facts emerge
in a cruel perversion of themselves. The keepers of the religious and
political establishment of the first century did not know the real
Jesus, we say. Yes, they saw the man and heard the words. They
knew of the healings and the teachings. They saw the cross and even
heard reports of the resurrection. But having eyes to see, they did not
see. Having ears to hear, they did not hear.

What kept them from knowing the real Jesus? Perhaps what
kept them from the real Jesus is keeping us from him too. It was not
that they were cynically immoral people, nor the victims of a per-
versity from which the rest of us are free. Rather they were misled
by a false belief that God had only spoken and acted in the past.
They were so concerned with preserving what God had said through
Moses and the prophets that they could not hear what he was saying
in their own time. They were so concerned with preserving the nation
God had called to be his own that they could not be open to the
kingdom of God that was coming.

The tragedy of the clash between Jesus and the establishment of his day was caused by what they firmly believed to be their virtues. To think that God was doing some great new work in their midst through Jesus had become an impossibility because of their loyalty to the past. Eyes were blinded because men looked backward to "the old-time religion." Their basic commitment to preserve the remnants of a disappearing past blinded them to the real Jesus.

The clash between Jesus and the religious and political leaders of his day throws a strong light on our own day. By one of those ironies of human history, faith in Jesus, once dangerously new, has become for us "the old-time religion." How do we describe the greatness of our churches? Too often, it is in terms of a glorious past. We like to glorify the revivals of the last century, the heroes of the Reformation, or the martyrs of the early church. We all love to sing lustily of the "Faith of Our Fathers." Yet is there not for us the danger of missing the real Jesus by simply clutching a disappearing past?

How then do we distinguish the good of the past from that which is merely old? How do we hold on to ancient truths and remain ever open to the voice of our risen, living Lord who *is* the truth?

2 | Jesus Between Revolution and Mysticism

The Pharisees, Sadducees, and priests were not the only ones who looked intently at Jesus. The revolutionary Zealots and the mystical Essenes each must have wondered if Jesus were really to be counted as one of them, if he would fulfill their hopes.

Living Between Politics and Piety

The Zealots and Essenes lived out a dedicated search for the better, more abundant life God promised his people. They were stirred by the very human longing for joy and freedom, for peace and hope, that lies in every one of us. They intensely wanted something more in life than the mere dreary round of existence with its drab boredom and grinding poverty. For both, their search for salvation was radical in its fervor, but their approaches to salvation were completely different. The Zealots wanted to establish the reign of God in the world by revolution, while the Essenes prepared themselves by mystical piety for the coming of the kingdom.

The Catholic philosopher Charles Péguy once said of the search for liberation that it always "begins in mysticism and ends in politics." Perhaps we could best say that the Zealots, on the contrary, started with politics. In their case, it was the politics of revolution. But they fervently hoped their search for salvation would end in mysticism. They believed their revolution would make the world a safe place in which to worship God. The Essenes did start with mysticism. They hoped that by their piety they could enter into a new world, where the only politics would be the kingdom of God.

It was this polarity, these opposite approaches to politics and piety, that formed the arena within which many people had to make

their decisions about Jesus. Their questions seem to have a ring of
the present day for us, for now, twenty centuries later, men and
women are still asking just how Jesus fits in between piety and
politics.

"Come the Revolution"

The longing to restore a glorious kingdom that recognized no
earthly power, but only the power of God, stirred the hearts of
countless Jewish people in Jesus' day. In their synagogues and homes
they told and retold the stories of the victorious battles of Moses
and Joshua, of Deborah and Gideon, of David and Solomon, and of
the Maccabees.

These great leaders of the past had a faith and daring that
God had rewarded. When they took up the sword, they did not
fight alone. The Lord himself fought with them. The frail authority
of the Sanhedrin that ruled first century Palestine by permission of
a Roman governor seemed a mockery of the glory that should be
Israel's.

Consequently, while the official leadership of the Jewish people
counselled submission and obedience, others secretly advocated
revolutionary violence. These underground revolutionaries were
known as Zealots. As their name proclaims, they were zealous for
the Lord and ready to be the agents of God's wrath against idolatry,
collaboration, and unbelief. A writer of that time cautioned, "There
are thousands of men keeping watch, Zealots of the Laws, strictest
guardians of the institutions of their fathers, merciless to those who
would do anything to subvert these."

The Zealots were, in part, a kind of self-appointed vigilante
committee, enforcing their own brand of justice. Assigning themselves
the role of surgeons excising a cancer, the Zealots believed their
sharp swords would rid Israel of the apostates that were bringing it
weakness and death. But the Zealots' faith lived out of a larger hope
than simply that of vengeance on the unfaithful or unpatriotic. They
dreamed of a day when their band would be joined by legions of
angels and be led by a warrior messiah to crush the Roman rule and
establish the kingdom of God on earth.

Rampant injustice, senseless violence, crushing taxes, and

endless exploitation had been the lot of the Jews long enough, they argued. They had evidence aplenty on their side. The Bible, for instance, tells of Herod's slaughter of the children (Matt. 2:16), and of the brutal cutting down of worshipers (Luke 13:1). The little people, the forgotten people of every age, our own included, feel themselves torn between hopeless resignation and a frenzy to strike back. No one who has ever trembled in silent rage at rank injustice or wanton cruelty can fail to feel a bit of the Zealot welling up in him. The big men have had the power long enough, they said, and now was the chance to seize the power that pliant high priests, crooked tax collectors, and proud landlords had taken away. Zealots were the revolutionary anti-establishment people who believed that only violence would accomplish their purposes.

The vision of the Zealots was never merely social or political or economic. Basically it was a vision of faith. They believed, as did many of their contemporaries, that an age was coming to an end. God had temporarily withheld his hand until his last great act which would smash injustice and establish the kingdom. They were standing at the very turning point of the ages. The Zealots lived with their eyes riveted on the future, straining to see the first sign that God was ready to act in final liberation. They would then strike in the full fury of their might, and, linked with the legions of angels, they would bring in the time of joy and peace.

The Zealots must have had their eyes on Jesus. One of their number, Simon the Zealot, had become a disciple (Luke 6:15). They wondered if Jesus were really the one sent from God to lead them to victory. He was a friend of the common man. He denounced the rich and the arrogant, and like the Zealots often spoke of the imminent coming of God's kingdom (as in Mark 1:15). Futhermore, the plotting of the religious and political establishment to silence Jesus marked him, in their eyes, as a man for revolution.

Yet Jesus perplexed them. They must have been confused by his talk about turning the other cheek, going the second mile, or forgiving enemies. What kind of a revolution, they must have wondered, could such words produce?

Then there came an act that seemed to mark Jesus as one of them. He went to the temple in Jerusalem at Passover time to find its courtyards crowded with merchants and money changers profiting on the sacrifices to be offered to God. He fashioned a whip of cords and drove them all out, overturning tables amid stampeding cattle and fluttering pigeons. As his disciples thought back on that scene of holy violence, they were reminded of the Psalmist's words, "Zeal for thy house will consume me" (John 2:17, Ps. 69:9). Such consuming zeal for holiness surely marked Jesus as a Zealot.

And what could be better for a revolutionary movement than to have the approval of this man who was so popular with the people? Their cause needed help, for many people had branded the Zealots as mere bandits and assassins. Could not Jesus give their movement the credibility it badly needed?

Yet, for all that cleansing of the temple meant, it did not seem the fully revolutionary act that would be the signal for God's war. So they still anxiously watched and waited. There was just a short step, they believed, between the stinging lash and their deadly swords. But would Jesus take that step? The arm of the Lord was about to be revealed, and it would be, for the Zealots, an arm holding the bloody sword of retribution. Was Jesus their messiah of violence?

Jesus too had searched the Scriptures. He too believed "the arm of the Lord" would soon be revealed, but on a cross, in suffering and death, and not in a sword causing suffering and death. The Zealots were doomed to disappointment.

Zealots In Our World

We still have Zealots in our midst today, though their titles have changed, and their weapons are no longer sword and dagger. The modern zealot is ready to argue that "justice grows out of a gun barrel." This slogan from Chairman Mao has stirred people in Asia, Latin America, and Africa, and has even resounded on our campuses and among our urban poor. The mythology may be different from that of the first century Zealots, but the reality remains the same: burn, destroy, overthrow, and a new world will emerge. Revolutionary movements have gripped men and women with a zeal in which they risk all in the present in hope for the future. We should not be surprised. When one's present life is drained of meaning, joy, or hope, the temptation to violence becomes very real. The rich of this world know the fear of revolution. The poor know the hope of revolution.

The coming of the Bicentenary in 1976 reminds us that the history of the United States, like that of ancient Israel, is marked by those who gained and preserved their freedom in the violence of battles. Sometimes violence is the birth pang of a better day, as in the American Revolution, but is it always? This is the difficult question for which there is no simple answer. But the gamble to try violence is not far from anyone whose life is one of exploitation and despair. And to this day people are anxious to have Jesus for their cause. So Jesus is pictured as the first real revolutionary, the liberator who freed people to live and who can make us free today.

Even those closest to Jesus were tempted to appeal to violence. When, after Peter's great confession of the Christ, Jesus tried to explain that the way of suffering and death was to be part of his messiahship, Peter would have none of it (Matt. 16:22). Not surprisingly, then, when Jesus was arrested in Gethsemane Peter fought (Matt. 26:51). People to this day keep on acting as if Jesus had praised Peter instead of rebuking him for wanting to defend him with violence. Jesus was clear—he needed no defending of that kind.

Something very dangerous happens to people when they start to think that their strength can make the world safe for God and his kingdom. When we feel our beliefs and values threatened, are we Christians not tempted ourselves in this way? We want to crush the opposition and be done with them, and all in the name of Jesus and for his sake. We want Jesus to be king of all who agree with us. When we feel those moods coming on, we should recall how, when the people sought during his earthly ministry to make Jesus king by force, he refused (John 6:15). The real Jesus would not become a messiah of violence.

The revolution of life of which Jesus spoke could never come at the point of a sword. Was this not what Jesus was saying in his admonition, "Put your sword back into its place; for all who take the sword will perish by the sword"? (Matt. 26:52) Jesus has had great difficulty with his followers, both ancient and modern, because they do not understand just what kind of a revolution it was that mankind was to undergo for its salvation. This is a question we must look at again in our own time. Certainly Jesus rejected the notion that the end to be accomplished justified the use of any means. Rather, Jesus seemed to be teaching that the means you use shape the kind of end you reach. Whether advocated by white citizens councils or by urban "liberationist armies" or by nationalistic militarism, hatred and violence seem only to create more hatred and violence rather than bring in the kingdom of God. Is it not true that any revolution is always in danger of destroying the very values it seeks to establish? The way to God's kingdom of love is still love. For, as Jesus taught with a kind of common sense ordinariness, "Are grapes gathered from thorns, or figs from thistles?" (Matt. 7:16) Hatred begets hatred, while love begets love.

Looking at the story of Jesus from the standpoint of the Zealots allows us to see some things clearly. Jesus *was* a strong leader who issued a forceful call for total commitment. He was unwilling to compromise with injustice, and he wanted none of his followers to compromise. Jesus had no program of gradualism. He did not come as a gentle persuader but as an imperious Lord, and so seemed to be the kind of man for whom the Zealots looked.

Yet the Zealots' vision of Jesus was twisted, for they did not see the real Jesus. They saw certain things about Jesus with wonderful clarity, yet they were blind to other things. The Zealots cannot be faulted for lack of passion or commitment or a willingness to sacrifice, virtues we so often find lacking in ourselves. And, unlike the leaders of the religious establishment of their day, they did not look backward to some imagined golden age of the past. Instead, their vision was focused on the future. They felt their present-day life and world were nearly bereft of God, so people and institutions could be treated with ruthless violence. Their faith was in a God who would come in the future, after the great revolution to overthrow Roman rule.

But their dreams of God's kingdom in the future kept them from seeing what God was doing in the present. The Zealots were blind to the immediate changes discipleship was bringing Jesus' followers. Jesus was a liberator. But the liberation he brought came as new life right then. Jesus knew that God had promised great things for the future, and Jesus' liberation is a power that has overcome not simply the tyranny of Rome but countless tyrannies ever since. Jesus also knew that God was doing great things in the present. People were undergoing revolutionary change—from being slaves of sin to being children of God. Changed themselves, they began to change everything about them. The question for us still remains: How open are we for this kind of a revolution?

The Mystic for All Times

Another group of people watched Jesus in ancient Palestine to see if he were the one they expected. They were the Essenes, whose name is not found in the New Testament. But with the finding of the Dead Sea Scrolls since World War II, we know a great deal more about this Jewish sect that was active in Jesus' time. Many of the people around Jesus had been touched by this strange group whose life centered in a monastery at Qumran near the Dead Sea. Perhaps John the Baptist had even been one of them.

The Essenes were a sect of Jewish people who had withdrawn to prepare themselves—in contemplation, study, and ritual purity—for the coming end of the world. The Essenes were revolted by the lust of the flesh and the vicious struggle of life. They wanted to be certain that when the final judgment came, they would be ready to stand before a righteous God free of compromise with the world. Their life was one of stern discipline, divided between worship and work.

Many of the followers of this sect lived in the villages of Palestine, only coming to Qumran to celebrate the Jewish holy day of Pentecost. Others were initiated into the inner life of the community and had left all worldly pursuits. They became celibate and followed complex rituals of prayer, fasting, washing for purification, and meditation. To enter the communal center at Qumran inspired awe in even the visitors. "To persons outside," an ancient writer recalled, "the silence of those within appears like some awful mystery." In this silence, people knew they were in the presence of the Holy. Each day there were hours of disciplined study of the Scriptures by minds attuned to God. These people were the mystics of Jesus' day.

The sacred books of the Essenes were filled with speculations about a teacher or prophet who would come at the end of the world.

As Jesus started his ministry of teaching and preaching, the eyes of many Essenes doubtless turned questioningly to him. Was he their expected one?

Jesus had, like many Essenes, turned from family and home to serve God. When Jesus' family came seeking him, he left them standing outside with words of startling severity. "Who are my mother and my brothers?" asked Jesus. "And looking around on those who sat about him, he said, 'Here are my mother and my brothers! Whoever does the will of God is my brother, and sister, and mother.' " (Mark 3:33-35) Here was a strictness of commitment that seems severe beyond understanding to us today. Yet to someone commited in deepest loyalty to God, all lesser loyalties dwindle in importance, and this was the very kind of strictness that the Essenes demanded of their members.

Also like the Essenes, Jesus rebuked the world and its rulers for their wickedness. His call to discipleship was so demanding that he warned, "the gate is narrow and the way is hard, that leads to life, and those who find it are few." (Matt. 7:14) Who understood this better than the Essenes, who had retreated from the world to prepare themselves for the last and terrible judgment of God? The easy optimism of our modern religion was as foreign to Jesus as it was to the Essenes. Eternity was a vast question that could only be answered by radical commitment and unswerving loyalty to God's will.

In addition, there was a deep thread of mystery that ran through Jesus' life. There was his time of contemplation and temptation in the wilderness after his baptism. There were those retreats into the hills for silent meditation and the early morning hours of prayer. So often in our reading of the New Testament we miss the importance of Jesus' life of contemplation. But this was not lost on the Essenes. Was not Jesus a man of mystic contemplation? These times of retreat, often into the very wilderness the Essenes found so dear in their own piety, surely made them wonder if he was not the one God had promised. Here was a man, people believed, who was submerged in the mystery of the Godhead. Jesus sounded to many people in that time, as well as our own times, like the teacher of a religion that led people away from the world to seek salvation in mystical piety.

The New Essenes

While the last of the Essenes died almost 2,000 years ago, something of their outlook is a part of life to this day. Before the turmoil of a revolution of hate and a reaction of fear, retreat from the world seems to many in our time to be the path of wisdom. Tired of the dispirited sterility of our traditional religions and of liturgies now dumb with age, we want a new consciousness of God, so traditional churches are being jostled by a search for a new piety. Mystical religion is also having a rebirth in our time as young people raised on secularism and materialism are turning to mysticism. The boredom, despair, and anger that erodes the center of life calls out for some deeper resource than can come from economic affluence or social status.

Consequently, many have turned to find some new forms of consciousness in religious sects that invoke Jesus or Krishna or Buddha. A host of new religious sects are springing up in our time. They all offer one basic thing: a new inner life of peace and joy. Perhaps these religious groups have touched your life or that of children or friends. People are seeking a mystic experience, be it found in a church or in the eastern cults now in our midst.

Not unrelated is the desire of others to remake our churches into sanctuaries of inner calm, where troubling thoughts of the world are left at the doorstep to be replaced by quiet organ music and calming words. We want the church to be a little retreat of quiet prayer amidst a world with which we can hardly cope. Today many people are turning from the churches whose preaching deals seriously with the injustices of modern society. The recent studies by sociologists of religion show this all too clearly. Twentieth century Americans want to leave social and political controversy at the door when they come to church. The religious group with rigid rules and ready answers seems an attractive retreat from a world where everything is perpetually "up for grabs." Is this not something we all feel at times? The Essene mentality is very much with us and our search for real life today. But is the real Jesus to be found here?

The Essenes did come close to touching the real core of Jesus' person. They knew that Jesus lived out of deep communion with God. They knew that faithfulness to God is expressed by a costly obedience to his will. But the Essenes missed the real Jesus because they believed God called them out of the world into a salvation of mystic bliss. The Essene mentality, both ancient and modern, is right in identifying Jesus as one who could be absorbed in mystic contemplation. Yet he turned from the rapture of contemplating God to bear the sins and sufferings of a clamorous world. Jesus always came back from the wilderness and down from the mountain top of transfiguration to people in their joys and sorrows. He returned to bear a cross. On the cross he died, not in the mystic's certainty of his place in the Godhead, but in the agony of a man who thought himself forgotten by God. He did this because he had come "not to be served but to serve, and to give his life as a ransom for many." (Mark 10:45)

With Jesus the path of contemplation did not lead to the wilderness. He did not dwell in the mystical experience or ecstatic excitement but in the world of everyday life. Mysticism misses the real Jesus because it looks for God only in the inner life or in the heavenly realms. The Essenes could not see what God was really doing through Jesus in their midst right then and there. The real mystery of Jesus was that God was working to reveal himself through this man amidst the clamor and folly of everyday life. By looking solely into the depth of our hearts or off into the beyond, we too may miss the real presence of God in this Jesus.

Neither Politics Nor Religion

At one time or another, we have all heard the quip about the man who was asked how he and his circle of friends got along so well together. He replied, "That's simple, we never talk about religion or politics."

It is evident that the language of politics is heavily freighted emotionally. Think of the reactions stirred by a serious discussion of words like "revolution," "law and order," "peace with honor," or "civil rights." We all have deeply felt values that can easily spill over into sharp, bitter divisions.

Religious words are even more troublesome at times. Think of the feelings stirred by opening our differences over words like "saved," "damned," or "baptism of the Holy Spirit," let alone words like "heathen," "heretics," "conservative," or "liberal."

Because we feel strongly on these issues, we tend to want to keep them to ourselves. We would like very much to keep our talk about Jesus free of all the troubling ideas and values that divide people. We are in the midst of what a sociologist once called "the privitization of religion." But in keeping our deepest thoughts and feelings to ourselves, we can also cut ourselves off from the struggle for truth in which the real Jesus can be met and known. In the first century, as in every century since in which people have found the real meaning of Jesus, they have found him in the midst of the toughest and most controversial issues of the day.

Jesus called men and women wherever he found them. He shrank from no person, no matter how partisan he or she might be. With the radical revolutionary, he spoke and acted against injustice and oppression; but he would have nothing of the mindless violence that sacrifices the present to an imagined future. Jesus knew with the Essenes the need for discipline and contemplation as pathways to God and to hope in life. But he rejected flight into the desert or into religious speculations about the schedule of God's plans for the future.

Jesus led people to make decisions about him who already had a loyalty to their political parties or their religious groups. He warned them, as he warns us, that commitment to him would create difficulties. Loyalty to him might not confirm what they had believed or thought. Loyalty to him always would lead them beyond where they had been to something new. Loyalty to him could drive wedges of separation between his followers and their friends and families.

Consequently, then and now, Jesus is rarely found by the lukewarm (Rev. 3:16), by those who avoid painful issues out of mistaken politeness. The search to find the truth about Jesus requires a kind of tough mindedness. Are our churches and Bible classes, our circle of families and friends willing to take these kinds of risks? Jesus then was found and today can be found in the midst of a world of revolution and a longing for mysticism. But he is calling people to something beyond either the revolution or the mysticism. He is calling people to a new kind of relationship with him. The New Testament has a word for it: "discipleship."

3

The Man
of the Spirit

There is something ironic about all those who did not
find the real meaning of Jesus because of the high regard in which
so many people held them. The Pharisee stood for the establishment,
pious and powerful. The Zealot was the champion of the oppressed
and the freedom fighter of his age. The Essene was the embodiment
of the mystical relationship to God we often say we long for, even
as it escapes us because of our lack of zeal.

Today their counterparts still have plenty of champions, both
in the church and in the world. In a time of confusion and uncertainty, who has not felt the tug of holding to a past-tense religion,
or the pressure to create a religion to bless and support our way of
life? Have you never dreamed of a future when God would crush
all oppressors and right all wrongs? At other times the religion of
dreamy otherworldliness seems the only option as the pain of life
rushes in.

Measured by the standards of a world that praises its Pharisees,
Zealots, Essenes, and their successors, the disciples seem an unlikely
crowd. The piety of our stained glass window saints misleads us.
To those left behind to run a fishing business, Peter and James
must have seemed irresponsible, while others thought them caught
up in a religious enthusiasm that bordered on madness. To the tax
collectors who looked forward to a rich retirement, Levi's sudden
departure must have seemed folly. What do you suppose was the
reaction of Chuza, King Herod's steward, when his wife Joanna left
home to accompany and help support Jesus and the twelve (Luke
8:1-3)?

Nor is it possible to admire the disciples because they always understood Jesus aright. After confessing Jesus to be the Christ, Peter was rebuked by Jesus because he wanted to claim him as a messiah of violence. When he revealed himself to Peter, James, and John on the mountain of transfiguration, they all wanted to stay there and enjoy their religious bliss, until Jesus forced them back down the mountain. The twelve squabbled over the power they expected to inherit when the Jesus-establishment replaced that of the Pharisees, priests, and Romans. Their formal doctrine of Christ seems sketchy by even the broadest standards of orthodoxy.

Becoming Disciples

What then marked these men and women as disciples? It was their willingness to open themselves in trust to Jesus. This was their faith. They were open to what God was doing in their midst through Jesus Christ. They did not measure Jesus solely in terms of what God had done in the past. They did not merely hope that God would do something through Jesus in the future. They trusted that through him God was starting to save right then. They were able to trust Jesus when he said, "You cannot tell by observation when the kingdom of God comes. There will be no saying, 'Look, here it is!' or 'there it is!'; for in fact the kingdom of God is among you." (Luke 17:21, NEB) They responded to the authoritative call of Jesus with what we take to be a careless suddenness. In faith they dropped their fishing nets, left their husbands, or turned from their tax tables as others watched in dumbfounded amazement.

How was such faith possible? The roads and hills of Palestine still seemed dusty, the sun hot, and the food scarce. Where was the kingdom in all of this? The kingdom of God was there, they started to realize, precisely because Jesus was there. He embodied that life-transforming power of God that would bring the life of the kingdom—joy, peace, hope, and love. By rejecting efforts to make themselves righteous by the laws of their religion, or to bring in the kingdom by force, or to find God in the wilderness through self-sacrificing piety, these disciples were ready to respond in faithful obedience to his claim on them. It was this willingness that allowed them to find the real Jesus.

Becoming a disciple of Jesus involves a break with your past. Jesus used the word "repentance" to talk about this break. Repentance involves far more than being sorry for some past misdeed. It is the about-face that Jesus asked of his original disciples. They had to see that what was required for new life was not a repair job, in which this or that unpleasant detail about them got changed. A whole new self was to come into existence. This was a transformation they could not bring about by themselves.

Jesus talked about the new self his disciples were receiving through relation to him in ways that seem startling, if not downright frightening, if taken seriously. "If any man would come after me, let him deny himself and take up his cross and follow me. For whoever would save his life will lose it, and whoever loses his life for my sake will find it." (Matt. 16:24-25, with parallels in all the Gospels) Such discipleship means a radical break with the old self that can only be called "death." So Paul described what happened to him as he became a disciple of Jesus: "I have been crucified with Christ; it is no longer I who live, but Christ who lives in me." (Gal. 2:20) This is total abandonment of what you are to become new in Christ.

A disciple, then, is one open and responsive to Jesus Christ and a radically new style of life. We have contrasted this way of discipleship with the more popular and respectable paths that others chose in Jesus' day, described in chapters 1 and 2. The question now arises, just what was it that people saw in Jesus that emboldened them to make this kind of response to him? How do you describe a person who could get other people to let their old selfhood wither and die, so that he could give them a new self? Fortunately, there is a word we can use—charisma.

The Man with Charisma

Many words are currently used to describe important people, to try to explain the basis of their appeal. We call them "dynamic" or "exciting"; even the word "beautiful" gets applied these days to male and female alike, to indicate not physical beauty as such, but personal style and power. At times admiration outstrips our vocabulary, as in the case of the young girl in the presence of her favorite pop singer. She exclaimed, "He's just WOW!"

A newly popular word has gained considerable currency in our vocabulary, the word "charisma." When trying to explain that finally elusive characteristic that makes a person compelling or important, we often conclude, "Well, you just have to say she's got charisma!" Charisma is a hard word to define because, as it has entered the vocabulary of TV commentators and newspapers, it has lost its religious roots and meaning. It commonly suggests personal power and charm, and the ability to awaken a response of hope and new energy. Originally, however, and as we are using it, it meant a great deal more.

"Charisma" comes from the Greek word for "grace." The plural form is found especially often in the New Testament and refers to the gifts of the Holy Spirit. So if we take the origins of the word "charisma" seriously, it would point to a person whose personal power is a gift, a gift of the Holy Spirit. This is not what is intended in most contemporary speech, but when we say now that Jesus had charisma, we mean primarily that he was Spirit-gifted. He was powerful, exciting, and winsome. The disciples, when they met Jesus, recognized him first of all as one with charisma.

It is hard for us to remember that when Jesus' first disciples met him they encountered no doctrine about him, nor did they meet an institution reared in his name. They accepted no creed; they joined no church. They simply met and followed one who came teaching, preaching, and healing. They were able to surrender themselves to him in faith because they sensed in him charisma: he was uniquely endowed with the spiritual gifts that come from the Holy Spirit. All too often we tend to think of the Holy Spirit solely as the one who came after Jesus rose and ascended. He did come at Pentecost to guide and empower the people of God, but the Gospel writers, especially Luke, present the person and ministry of Jesus with frequent references to the Holy Spirit. Presumably it was this power of the Spirit in and through Jesus that first awakened the response of faith in his disciples, for it is the Spirit who has the power to produce new spiritual life (John 3:5-8).

The Gospel writers did not relate the Spirit to the coming of

Jesus simply as a bit of interesting history. They saw in this fact the clue to how people were changed through their relation to Jesus.

The Gospel of John sets it forth as a contrast: "That which is born of the flesh is flesh, and that which is born of the Spirit is spirit." (John 3:6)

Let's start with the first part of the contrast, "That which is born of the flesh is flesh." Whenever we start out to do something, our success is limited by our own powers and abilities. Human powers are great, as we well know in this age of technology. We can go to the moon and beyond. We can move rivers and mountains. We can wrest energy from the atom. We can heal broken bodies. But the one thing human power cannot give us is new life, a fresh start. This is a gift that comes from the Spirit of God. "That which is born of the Spirit is spirit." The Spirit sets in motion the new beginning for humanity through Jesus, and it was through Jesus that the Spirit would enter human life ever afterward.

To ground Jesus' ministry in the work of the Spirit also shows that it is not a kind of human success story. In what was happening through Jesus Christ, God himself had taken the initiative. This is why so much talk about Jesus being "just a very good man and a great teacher" is so wide of the mark. Such a vision of Jesus brings us right back to John's words, "that which is born of the flesh is flesh." That which comes from some human powers can do all that a person can do, but not what the Spirit can do. If Jesus were only a good and great teacher, he could probably teach us many fine and helpful things. Yet he could not bring us the new being that we really need. "That which is born of the Spirit is spirit." It is Jesus as the unique bearer of the Spirit who empowers us to turn from the old and to get new life from him. To have a self-abandoning trust in Jesus, the disciples found, was to be made new by the Spirit.

Jesus no human success story

Jesus then was uniquely the man with charisma, and to see the story of his life in this light may show us more clearly how the Spirit is living and working today.

At Birth and Baptism, the Spirit

There is a striking parallel in the emphasis on the Holy Spirit at the beginnings of the Old Testament and of the New. When

*H.S.
beyond
of N.T.*

creation got its start, Genesis tells us that "the Spirit of God was moving over the face of the waters." (Gen. 1:2) Then, as the new creation got its start in Jesus Christ, the Spirit again moved with wonderful power. The conception of Jesus was by the power of the Holy Spirit (Matt. 1:18, 20; Luke 1:35). The birth of Jesus' forerunner, John the Baptist, was surrounded by the work of the Spirit (Luke 1:41-79). The aged prophet Simeon was inspired by the Spirit to recognize and bless the infant Jesus (Luke 2:25-35).

The Gospel records of Jesus' public ministry in first century Palestine start with his baptism by John. It is always tempting to speculate about what Jesus may have thought or felt at the time of his baptism and the dramatic events that followed from it. However, the New Testament gives us little evidence for such guess-work. Rather, it centers attention in the baptism narratives on one fact: The Spirit came upon Jesus in his baptism. (See Matthew 3:13-17, with its parallels.) This was the time of empowering, when Jesus was made ready for the mighty acts of teaching, preaching, healing, driving out of demons, and giving of new life that were to follow. Nor was this gift of the Spirit some fleeting high point of religious experience. It was an abiding power given to Jesus. In the words of John the Baptist, "I saw the Spirit descend as a dove from heaven, and it remained on him." (John 1:32) Here Jesus received the charisma for his public ministry.

*H.S. at
Jesus'
baptism
&
stayed.*

In sharp contrast to our usual expectations, the gift of the Spirit and the designation of Jesus as the well-beloved Son did not lead to a time of bliss and peace. Instead, it led to sharp and dangerous conflict. "The Spirit immediately drove him into the wilderness. And he was in the wilderness forty days, tempted by Satan; and he was with the wild beasts." (Mark 1:12-13) The whole temptation narrative is hard for us to understand. For instance, just why would the Spirit lead Jesus to this time of testing? Yet Mark puts it more strongly; the Spirit *drove* him, he says. The traditional image we have of the gifts of the Holy Spirit is of comfort, joy, and peace. But in the case of Jesus, immediately he was put to the test: Would he misuse these great powers?

*Spirit led
Jesus.*

In the temptations of Jesus, we touch one of the deepest ambiguities of the spiritual life. People can take their gift of leader-

Jesus did not use power for himself

ship, authority, and power—in other words, their charisma—and misuse it. This is why there is always an ambiguity in the usual use of the word "charisma." To say a person has charisma, in the profane sense, may mean he or she has the key not only for good, but also for selfish gain and for the exploitation of any who follow. Human history is filled with the ruin of people who have blindly followed charismatic leaders who have betrayed the trust their followers have placed in them.

This possibility was open to Jesus. He was tried by a three-fold temptation to misuse his miraculous power and authority. When Jesus rejected the temptation to pervert these powers for selfish ends, he was ready for his ministry. Before he could call others to receive the Spirit from him, Jesus' gift was tested and refined. Jesus returned from the temptation "full of the Holy Spirit" and ready to start his public ministry.

The Spirit and the Ministry of Jesus

The use of the word "ministry" to characterize Jesus' work may be confusing for people today. We tend to picture the minister as a teacher and preacher or as one particularly concerned with the sick and distressed of his congregation. So far, this gives a good clue to Jesus' ministry. But to the measure that the minister also is seen as the one fretted and harrassed by committee meetings, building fund drives, and the like, the picture is of course misleading.

In its origins, the word "ministry" means a work of service to others. Mark wrote, Jesus "came not to be served but to serve" (Mark 10:45), and the Gospels show him so doing. But a minister is also "a person acting as the agent or instrument of another." A government sends its "minister" to another country to speak and act on its behalf. A ruler may send a "minister" to act for him in delicate negotiations. The minister acts on the basis of the power of the one he represents.

Ministry: work for another

This second meaning of the word "minister" may give us some idea of how the disciples first encountered and understood Jesus. Jesus was the one acting and speaking for God in the power of the Holy Spirit. His work of healing and driving out of demons was done in the power of the Spirit. In fact, Jesus warned against attributing his powers to anyone save the Holy Spirit.

One thing seemed very clear to both Jesus' friends and foes. He had unusual powers to heal and transform human lives. In the modern world we are tremendously skeptical about miracles. Such was not the case in Jesus' own day. The argument was not over whether the mighty acts had happened or not. The question was over how Jesus accomplished them. Jesus' opponents held that the power behind his mighty works was evil, and that his aim was selfish. Against this view, Jesus used a simple argument. Evil forces cannot bring forth a good result. Satan is the father of lies and death, so he can never be the source of healing and hope. Through Jesus the Spirit bore the fruits of the Spirit.

Jesus pressed the point still further. It was the Holy Spirit who was working through him in the mighty acts of his ministry. To deny this, Jesus said, was extremely dangerous. "And whoever says a word against the Son of man will be forgiven; but whoever speaks against the Holy Spirit will not be forgiven, either in this age or the age to come." (Matt. 12:32) Personal denial of Jesus could be forgiven, as it was in the case of Peter. But denial of the Spirit's working through Jesus reveals a kind of ultimate moral and spiritual blindness. It seals people off from salvation because it is the denial of how God works in this world for human salvation. To get confused at this point, to call good evil and evil good, is permanently to join the ranks of those "who have eyes to see, but see not, and ears to hear but hear not." Disciples, in contrast, are those who rejoice in the way the Spirit is working through Jesus. Disciples of every age see in these mighty acts the fulfillment of the promises of God through the prophets of old. (See the Biblical quotation in the next paragraph for an example of such a promise.)

The Spirit was also the source of the teaching and preaching of Jesus. When Jesus got up in the synagogue in Nazareth to preach, he began by quoting Isaiah 61, "The Spirit of the Lord is upon me, because he has anointed me to preach good news to the poor. He has sent me to proclaim release to the captives and recovering of sight to the blind, to set at liberty those who are oppressed, to proclaim the acceptable year of the Lord." (Luke 4:18-19) By this and other preaching and teaching, men and women were led to respond in faith to God and to Jesus himself. Did Jesus speak by the power of the Spirit or not? To decide that it was the Spirit who spoke through Jesus was the first step towards living in the power of the Spirit.

We have seen that a key mark of a disciple was being open and responsive to Jesus, rather than choosing one of the alternate patterns of commitment of the Pharisees, Zealots, or Essenes that are similar to ones still popular today. The disciples responded in faithful obedience because they saw in Jesus charisma—not just charm and power, but the gift of the Holy Spirit. The work of the Holy Spirit in Jesus' life started before his birth. At his baptism he received the Spirit in a new way for ministry, and in his temptation he decided how he would use his gifts. By the power of the Holy Spirit he carried out his ministry, and by that power people were led to respond to him in faith.

H. S. Through Jesus to Disciples

Then, after the early disciples began to follow Jesus, something strange and wonderful started to dawn on them: In their relationship to Jesus they were slowly, but nonetheless really, becoming more like him. The power that was at work in him was starting to work in them also. For his own part, Jesus put the matter with startling clarity: "Truly, truly, I say to you, he who believes in me will also do the works that I do; and greater works than these will he do. . . ." (John 14:12) From the Book of Acts and from many later pages in the history of the church, it is clear that disciples of Jesus started to share in this new power and life in dramatic ways. They too had charisma.

All of this opens for us the question, Do Christians today receive the gifts of the Holy Spirit, and, if so, how, and what gifts?

Every Christian a Charismatic!

The question just stated has a new currency today, since many Christians are seeking to find the meaning of spiritual gifts and the work of the Spirit through the spread of the so-called "charismatic movement," with its emphasis on speaking in tongues and faith healing.

We have to reach to John the Baptist and his prophecy about Jesus to understand this issue. John the Baptist drew a contrast between what he was doing and what the Christ would do. "I baptize you with water for repentance . . . He will baptize you with the Holy Spirit." (Matt. 3:11) John was doing something that was absolutely essential. By his baptism for repentance, he was calling men and women to that first vital form of self-awareness that makes receiving Jesus Christ as Lord a possibility. He was calling them to repent, to turn away from their present way of life and toward God.

Repentance is learning to ask the right questions about yourself. It is learning to lay bare before God the persistent self-interest and pride that corrupts our best efforts at love and understanding. Unless a person is able to do that, he or she will never be able to make much sense of the radical call to discipleship that comes from Jesus.

But no matter how vital this beginning is, it is still a dim, temporary preparation for something greater that is to come. The Christ "will baptize you with the Holy Spirit." Repentance is still necessary, but what has happened through Jesus transforms this start made in repentance into something infinitely greater. It is life by the Spirit.

The early church had some people that had taken the first step—the baptism of John for repentance—but had not gone any further. Apollos and some unnamed disciples at Ephesus had not been baptized with the Holy Spirit (Acts 18:24; 19:7). Their religion was one only of moral earnestness and, at least in the case of Apollos, of intellectual brilliance. But Apollos had to be taught "the way of God" more accurately by Priscilla and her husband Aquilla, while the unnamed disciples, after being instructed about Jesus by Paul, "were baptized in the name of the Lord Jesus." This enabled them to enter that newness of life Jesus offered.

The crucial thing to remember in these incidents is that the Spirit is not reserved for a special group. "God gives him the Spirit without reserve." (John 3:34, JB) He belongs to all disciples simply because they are disciples; discipleship is his work. The inner work of the Spirit is that process of life in which the old self dies and the new self comes into being. Jesus, *the* one with charisma, gives to his disciples "the spiritual gifts," the *charismata*. This is not simply God's provision for some spiritual elite, it is his way of dealing with all the disciples of Jesus. The Chinese Christian leader, Watchman Nee, has a wonderful phrase to characterize this new life in the Spirit. He calls it "the normal Christian life." Every Christian is a charismatic, though not all Christians have the same charismatic gifts.

Are we open to these powers that transform and renew life? Are we open to the Holy Spirit? This is the kind of question that the retelling of the encounter of Jesus with his disciples forces on anyone who is open to discipleship today. In the introduction to his translation of Acts, J. B. Phillips puts the question sharply:

> But we cannot help looking wistfully at the sheer spiritual power of the minute young Church, which was expressed not only by healing the body but "by many signs and wonders" which amply demonstrated the fact that these men were in close touch with God.
>
> Of course it is easy to "write off" this little history of the Church's first beginnings as simply an account of an enthusiastic but ill regulated and unorganized adolescence, to be followed by a well disciplined maturity in which embarrassing irregularities no longer appear. But that is surely too easy an explanation altogether. We in the modern Church have unquestionably *lost* something. Whether it is due to the atrophy of the quality which the New Testament calls "faith," whether it is due to a stifling churchiness, whether it is due to our sinful complacency over the scandal of a divided Church, or whatever the cause may be, very little of the modern Church could bear comparison with the spiritual drive, the genuine fellowship, and the gay unconquerable courage of the Young Church.[1]

4

The Violence of the Cross

So far we have pictured the contrast between the path of Christian discipleship and the often more popular paths of preserving the establishment, of revolutionary violence, or of withdrawal —four different ways to try to cope with or confront the world and its threats and opportunities. We have gone on to describe the way of discipleship as a response to the charismatic (Spirit-gifted) Jesus, a response marked by a willingness on the part of the first disciples to be open to new challenges and to change.

We have seen that when they responded, the Holy Spirit, who made faith possible, worked to bring about their increasing Christlikeness. The New Testament says that the same is true of today: every Christian can rightly be called a charismatic, one who has the gifts of the Spirit, though Christians differ from one another in the particular gifts they are given.

For the first disciples, transformation came in Palestine as they responded to the Jesus who called them to follow him. Two thousand years later, people are still being transformed by responding to Jesus. We do not meet him on the hills of Galilee or in the streets of Capernaum. Instead, many of us were first touched by a grisly scene of violence—a cross outside a city wall.

The Meaning of This Death

Violence is a fact of our time. We are preoccupied with the violence that haunts the city streets, destroys life in wars, and maims human spirits with its threat. By contrast, we think of Christianity in terms of tranquility and peace. However, at its center stands an act of violence. This act is symbolized by the best-known emblem of the faith, the cross.

The death of Jesus was a terrible act. Years of Christian piety have covered the brute fact of that violent death with a kind of veneer, like the gold with which we plate our crosses. But the sheer horror remains. It was not simply another tragedy of human history. It was a tragedy that demanded that people try to make sense of it. How can we keep faith in a loving and powerful God in the face of the death of his Son?

The tragedy of Jesus' death had its origins in his ministry. Jesus by his very presence seemed to call people to make a decision about him. Part of the story of those decisions has already been traced. It is written by those disciples, ancient and modern, who opened themselves to Jesus and found in him the working of the Spirit of God.

But if a decision is a real one, it always implies that some people will answer "no." From early in his ministry there was a growing wave of opposition to Jesus. According to Mark, plotting against Jesus started with his mighty acts of healing and teaching: "The Pharisees went out, and immediately held counsel with the Herodians against him, how to destroy him." (Mark 3:6) The story of Jesus and his disciples was to be written in terms not only of a growing awareness of his lordship, but also of growing opposition and violence.

The historical outline of his death is already well-known. A self-interested religious and political hierarchy stirred the passions of a mob to bring about an execution that was nothing but a judicial murder. Roman justice bent under the pressure of a crowd. Jesus' death was brought on by a torture that made his body, in fact, "a broken body," the victim of scourging, thorn and nail wounds, and slow strangulation.

But it was a death of more than sheer physical violence. Death on the cross put its victim under a curse. As the ancient Scriptures taught, "cursed be everyone who hangs on a tree." (Deut. 21:23; Gal. 3:13) Jesus, whom his followers believed had come "to redeem Israel," died cast out by state and by church. Measured in these terms, Paul was right in saying "Christ crucified, a stumbling block to Jews and folly to the Gentiles." (1 Cor. 1:23) Yet in almost the next breath Paul vows "to know nothing among you except Jesus Christ and him crucified," because this crucified Christ is "the power of God and the wisdom of God." How did an act of human violence become the source of salvation? This is the mystery of the cross.

Christians have tried to explain this mystery in many ways. God's reconciling act in Jesus Christ is called by Scripture the sacrifice of a lamb, a shepherd's life given for his sheep, atonement by a priest, the ransom of a slave, the payment of a debt, vicarious satisfaction of a legal penalty, or the victory over the powers of evil. People have used these various ways to characterize what happened on the cross because no human words are fully adequate. The power and love of God are seen in the cross because it is the symbol of a death that has brought life to mankind. Whenever we try to speak of life coming through a death, our ordinary ways of thinking are confounded. Ordinarily we say that death is the abolition of life. How can Christians say life has come from his death?

For the earliest disciples this was not some vague theological issue to be argued about intellectually. They faced this question with startling reality. They had cut themselves off from all their old centers of hope—from family and jobs and traditional religion. They had hoped that "he was the one who should redeem Israel." But with his death all these hopes seemed dashed. What sense were they —or we—to make of it?

The best human answer to the meaning of the cross by itself is to see it as a martyrdom: Jesus died for his ideals. Such a vision of self-sacrifice can possibly inspire us to good and great actions, and there is truth here. Jesus lived in the wonderful freedom of those who follow their vision of the good with carefree abandon. He could not be coerced. He lived this way because he was willing to accept the ultimate power evil has over good—its power to take the life of the person of good will.

However, disciples have never settled for this picture of Jesus' death, no matter how noble it seems. The picture of Jesus the Martyr fails because it leaves Jesus dead in his grave. His memory may inspire, but his mission failed. The disciples saw the cross as a victory because they viewed it in light of his risen presence. Something happened with Jesus Christ that is unique in human life: a person was raised from the dead. And because of this, the very meaning of death itself was changed.

Gaining and Losing Life

Jesus gave a key to the meaning of the cross when he said, "Whoever cares for his own safety is lost; but if a man will let himself be lost for my sake, he will find his true self." (Matt. 16:25, NEB) Human life is threatened on every hand. Early in life most of us learn to obey the traffic light and avoid the rickety ladder, but no amount of caution ever seals us off from all the threats posed by life.

More serious than physical threats are the forces of guilt, fear, loneliness, suffering, and death. We find it difficult to give ourselves to others in friendship or love because to open one's self to someone else risks the pain of rejection. We do not ever really enjoy ourselves because we fear the joy won't last. Like the one talent servant in Jesus' parable (Matt. 25:14-30), we withdraw into ourselves to preserve what little there is of us. But, as Jesus said, such a person not only is not secured from threat, he is the victim of total loss. "Whoever cares for his own safety is lost."

We try to seek our own safety in this world by economic might, military power, social prestige, or political influence. Are not these schemes of ours forever frustrated? Military might has not brought national security; we know only national insecurity. A record "gross national product" leaves us still struggling to make ends meet. Social cliques quickly become sore little groups of people unable to enjoy themselves because they are so busy excluding others. The parent who so desperately wants to save a child from harm can easily cut him off from real growth, be it the baby taking his first steps or a teenager on her first date. "Whoever cares for his own safety is lost."

Jesus lived amidst threats that finally brought about his death. Yet he lived in the glorious liberty of one who did not seek his own safety. He was willing to let himself be lost for the sake of the kingdom of God. The result was an ever-heightening conflict with those who rejected discipleship. His enemies slandered him, threatened him, and finally used the ultimate coercion—death. He accepted this rather than saving himself by rejecting what God had called him to do in the world.

Jesus had a disciple whom he knew would betray him. Yet Jesus remained open to Judas, inviting him into the intimacy of his Last Supper with his disciples. Judas cut himself off from Jesus, but Jesus never cut himself off from Judas. Jesus had the freedom to live in an open relationship even with his betrayer. Jesus lived in this freedom because he found his true self rooted and grounded in God. Living this way ultimately brought him to the cross. But Jesus was willing to go to the cross because he knew that the only real safety is to live in openness to others. To stay turned in on yourself is not life, but only physical existence.

Luther used a fascinating phrase to talk about sin. He said that man in sin is "curved in upon himself." The sinner is the person who by rejecting the love of God is left "curved in upon himself," trying to shield himself from the threats and fears that assail him. This is not life but existence, like a kind of spiritual ingrown toenail.

Death on the cross did not destroy the true self Jesus had in God. If he had turned from the cross by compromising on his mission, he might have lived, but his true self would have been lost. Jesus' acceptance of death on the cross was an act of faith in God and God's willingness to save those who risk giving themselves to others in love. In the resurrection God vindicated Jesus' act of faith. The death and resurrection of Jesus Christ means that his call to live in self-giving love toward others is not just an idealist's theory, appealing but untried. Jesus made it a fact of human life.

The Supreme Identity

The cross stands at the center of the Christian message because it is the point of supreme identity of God with human beings. Jesus Christ has not only assumed our humanity, he has also taken upon himself our sin and death. Paul explained what God was doing through Jesus in this way. "For our sake he made him to be sin who knew no sin, so that in him we might become the righteousness of God." (2 Cor. 5:21)

The shocking force of this verse is hard to grasp. It somehow seems possible to conceive of God identifying with what is good and great. But to say he has accepted in Jesus Christ human sin and has died because of this sin is an extravagrance for which we are not prepared.

Our natural tendency has always been to make salvation a "do-it-yourself" project. The basic human plan for salvation runs something like this: "Seeing the disadvantages of sin, we are trying to stop sinning. While we may not be perfect, we are doing as well as can be expected." It offends us to think that someone else had to take the responsibility for our sin. Yet this is what stands at the heart of the Christian message about the cross. Jesus Christ has died our death so that we may live his life. The words are frighteningly clear. He became sin; he became a curse. He entered into the fear, alienation, guilt, and pain that is sin.

The cross of Christ makes it clear that in dealing with human sin God forgives us, he does not just indulge us. This distinction is important. We cannot stand the tension of a broken relationship and, seeking real reconciliation, we try to push the offense aside or to act as if it had never happened. In a kind of strained politeness we indulge one another's sins no matter how deeply they have hurt.

This is not forgiveness. No reconciliation can follow from it. This is a false indulgence that tries to take sin lightly. It is a violation of justice that ignores the way in which sins, even so-called "little sins," destroy community and destroy people.

God never makes this mistake in dealing with sin. He is a just God. His very being is justice. His forgiveness does not come from his ignoring the demands of the law; this would let the world lapse into moral chaos. It comes from the demands of justice being fulfilled. Sin comes at a terribly high price. This is why our world is the way it is today. Forgiveness is possible because someone else has paid that price for us.

Throughout his life Jesus identified himself with the burden of human guilt. In his baptism, the sinless one willingly identified himself with sinners. On the cross, he took the final step of identification: "Christ was without sin, but God made him share our sin that we, in union with him, might share the righteousness of God." (2 Cor. 5:21, TEV)

Such forgiveness leads to healing. It is the basis on which a whole world can be reconciled with God. We should notice very carefully what Paul said about this reconciliation: "God was in

Christ reconciling the world to himself." (2 Cor. 5:18, NEB) He does not say that God has been reconciled to the sinfulness of his creatures. It is the other way around. People are being reconciled to God by the forgiveness granted in Jesus Christ. In other words, the world is being made new.

Forgiveness is restoring the broken relationship between God and us. It never merely looks backward to the wiping out of past sins. It also creates the possibility for a new future. Forgiveness is the basis of reconciliation. It is the grounds for new relationships among people. This reconciliation is never just a private or personal thing. It reaches out to a whole world that needs reconciliation. It touches the world with its broken relations between young and old, white and black, the silent majority and the talkative minorities, the urban ghetto and the suburban club. This reconciliation can mean the healing of nations, and its outcome is the kingdom of God.

Dying and Rising with Christ

It has never been possible to speak of the death and resurrection of Christ simply in the past tense, as if it were something over and done with. His death and resurrection have a continuing power to shape life. When we try to take them seriously, we can feel Paul's words, "I have been crucified with Christ: the life I now live is not my life, but the life which Christ lives in me;" or "For if we have become incorporate with him in a death like his, we shall also be one with him in a resurrection like his." (Gal. 2:20, NEB; Rom. 6:5, NEB) What Paul was saying is that the power for human beings to find their true selves by losing their old selves has been let loose in the world by Jesus Christ.

What we now are—selves trying to be secure without God—is crucified with Christ. When we live by faith, we start to experience this dying to the old self. The values and hopes we had fashioned for ourselves, even the fear and doubts that dogged our steps, start to lose their grip on us. The hatreds and the possessiveness that distort our efforts to love have been brought to an end. In their place, a new life is starting to spring up. It is resurrection life. It is new being that allows us to reach out and share the life of another. It is "I, yet not I, but Christ who dwells in me."

This dying and rising is not as strange as it at first sounds. Instead, it is very basic to being human. When two people marry, they die to the freedom to come and go at will. Neither can they any longer think solely of "I"; each must now think of "we." In doing this, they enter into a new and richer life.

The previously all-white church that admits blacks to its membership dies to the social solidarity it had in its all-white culture. It has to take into account people who worship differently and want different things from their church. Yet the church is resurrected into a fuller life.

When children start to school, they die to the possibility of sleeping till 11:00 a.m. or watching TV at 1:00 p.m. They have to be in school to learn so they may enter a fuller life.

This is what it means to be raised to newness of life. We have to die to the all-too-human willingness to reshape the truth to suit our own needs, in order to live in honesty with one another. We have to die to half-truths, even when they please us, to be resurrected into the real world. We need to die to a false national pride that is very literally killing some of us, to be resurrected into peace for the world. We need to die to the freedom to litter, pollute, and poison nature, to be resurrected into a world of ecological balance. The drug addict has to die to that demonically fascinating world of psychedelic colors and sounds, in order to be raised to the new world of sanity, peace, and wholeness.

What Christian faith means in all of these struggles is that we can enter them in the power of one who has died and been raised already. By living in Christ, we joyfully confess that all these forms of the old self have been nailed to a cross and have died. Disciples of Christ have found they were finished and done with the old life. We start to enter into the resurrection life through Christ. Paul caught the meaning of this dying and rising with Christ when he wrote, "His purpose in dying for all was that men, while still in life, should cease to live for themselves, and should live for him who for their sake died and was raised to life." "When anyone is united to Christ, there is a new world; the old order has gone, and a new order has already begun." (2 Cor. 5:15 and 17, NEB)

Perhaps a question has entered your mind at this point. Does not seeing the Christian life as dying and rising with Christ mean a joyless and drab existence? Too often Christians have thought that dying to self meant the suppression of happiness. Christians have tended to think that dying with Christ implied the bleak austerity of the medieval monastery or the dour self-denial of a distorted puritanism. It seemed as if some believed they would be assured of joy in heaven only if they had no joys on earth.

Salvation is *not* our reward for giving ourselves over to a life of discomfort. To be sure, there is pain to the dying of the old nature in us. To touch the depth of our own self-righteous pride or to wrestle with the power of our sinful desires is a very real pain. Joy comes in realizing that *we* do not have to overcome the old. Jesus Christ has done this already. The resurrection into newness of life is already a fact. By faith we start to enter into it now. In hope we look forward to the completion of that joy with confidence. So we can confess that "in our sorrows we have always cause for joy; poor ourselves, we bring wealth to many; penniless, we own the world." (2 Cor. 6:10, NEB)

The lay theologian Friedrich von Hugel calls this new life received in dying and rising with Christ "Supernatural Life." He does not mean by this that the new life is somehow strange or spooky. It is supernatural because it comes from a power beyond that of which we are capable as natural men and women.

The cross of Christ is the story of a rescue of humankind from the power of sin and death. But it is more. It is the story of the release of that supernatural life of joy into the world. At the cross, Jesus did not stop to count the cost or reckon with the worth of those for whom he died. His dying and rising took all of us in our ordinariness and opened the way into the kingdom. The final word about the Christian life is not the word "sad" but the word "joy." And the root of this joy is not our accomplishments but God's gift.

How can such an interpretation of the significance of Jesus' death be helpful to you? What further questions do you have? Do you recall the story of the death of Jesus Christ on the cross having influenced any conscious decision about him that you have made?

5

No Disciples
at Second Hand

Perhaps you have started to note in this book a kind of unspoken assumption. Now is the time to take a hard look at it.

In retelling the story of Jesus and the people who were closest to him, both friend and foe, we have seen an intimate link between his times and our own. Thus, when learning of the struggle to know Jesus aright in the first century, we have been told something of our struggle to know him aright amid the religious, social, and political pressures of the twentieth century. When retelling the story of his life lived in the power of the Spirit, it became evident that he is still the key to the gift of the Spirit in our own times. When finding the meaning of his death on the cross, we start to discover what his cross means in life today. What makes possible this kind of approach to Jesus which links past with present?

To put the question another way, it may be all well and good to show how Peter, Mary Magdalene, and the rest became disciples, but how about us? How can we in the twentieth century ever enter into that faithful trust in Jesus that makes people his disciples? To say that the kingdom of God was present in his person may have been great for those first century Jews that saw him, but how do we make our decisions about him? An eloquent preacher or a skilled writer can bring New Testament people alive in our imagination, but is there a reality in all this that can enter our lives? Is Jesus ever my contemporary, so that I can enter into a personal relationship with him?

The answers to these questions are linked together in one affirmation: Jesus Christ was raised from the dead. The Christian faith comes to a unique focus in the resurrection of Christ. To say that Jesus is the risen one is to say, among other things, that he is free to be alive and at work in the world and in our lives today.

Søren Kierkegaard, a Christian teacher of the last century, caught the importance of the resurrection for our faith in saying that there is no such thing as "a disciple at secondhand." What did he mean by that? We all realize that someone else's testimony or historical information may be of help. But neither can be a final guarantee of the reality of Jesus and his power to give me life. If we are to be disciples at first hand, then Jesus has to be alive in our midst. We cannot have a personal relationship with ideas about Jesus or with an institution reared in his name. If discipleship is a possibility for us, it is because Jesus is alive.

When the early Christians affirmed the resurrection of Jesus, they were not saying that he had gone safely to heaven to await us there. The resurrection places Jesus on this side of the grave, in the here and now of everyday life, awaiting our response to him. The resurrection of Jesus is not a kind of added extra to underline the importance of his ethics or to enhance his influence over people, nor is it a sort of inspired guess which Christians make about the importance of Jesus. Rather, the resurrection is the basic reality out of which Christian faith grows. The resurrection of Christ is the basis for our responding to him here and now. In faith we are not touching an idea or a remembrance, we are sharing in the life of another person.

Trying to Find the Facts

To put the resurrection of Jesus at the heart of our approach to him is to make central that claim for Christian faith that has been most often questioned and rejected. Many say they are willing to accept the moral example of Jesus but must leave the resurrection claim aside. But to seek the real Jesus honestly, it is necessary to examine the claims for him at just this point with care. Is the resurrection of Jesus from the dead fact or fantasy? The question is unavoidable because in our relationship with God we dare not live out of illusions.

The argument against the resurrection has been stated in many ways. It usually reduces itself to a simple point. Since dead people remain dead, any report of one rising from the dead must not be true. The reports of the disciples that Jesus was raised from the dead must be, it is argued, wishful thinking, illusion, or fraud.

The average churchgoer dismisses this kind of thinking as impiety. Yet this hardly settles the matter. A growing number of people, within and outside the churches, have concluded that belief in a risen Jesus is simply not possible. Magazine articles and paperback books parade before us the findings of so-called "scientific historians" who say the resurrection of Jesus was a misunderstanding. The simple "put-down" that brushes this all aside as nastiness and unbelief is not a very convincing rebuttal or positive testimony to the truth.

Three historical facts stand at the heart of the Christian proclamation of the resurrection of Jesus: (1) Jesus actually died on the cross. (2) He was later seen alive by his disciples. (3) On the third day after his death his tomb was empty.

One of the oft-recurring ways to explain the empty tomb and the appearance of Jesus is the argument that he never really died on the cross; he simply went into a deep swoon or trance. The "resurrection" was only Jesus' being resuscitated. As unlikely as this argument may seem, it has been used by some historians to explain the resurrection of Jesus. Most recently it appeared as the finding of Hugh Schonfield in his book, *The Passover Plot.* Jesus had been drugged at the time of crucifixion, the book claims, so the seemingly dead Jesus could "rise" later when he revived.

One problem with this argument is that Jesus rejected the very wine mixed with myrrh that could have drugged him against the agony of crucifixion (Mark 15:23). The cheap, sour wine offered him later had no purpose save to satisfy momentarily his thirst (Mark 15:36).

Nor can it be argued that six hours on the cross would not produce death. Many who were crucified were fastened tightly against the cross, often with a small platform for their feet. These unfortunates did often linger for a day or two before they finally died from loss of blood and body fluids. Others, and this seems to have been the case with Jesus, died in a matter of hours because their bodies were only held to the cross by the nails. In this case, the victim could not long hold himself erect. When he slumped forward on the cross, he was forced to carry the full weight of his body on his arms. This led to strangulation in a relatively short time. Jesus thus could well have died in six hours from shock and strangulation. The spear thrust into his side let out not only blood but also fluid that had probably started to fill his lungs (John 19:34).

The resuscitation theory goes on to declare that Jesus revived after being placed in the tomb. The notion that being placed in a cool tomb or having the body covered by embalming spices could so revive Jesus that his disciples would think him fully restored to life makes this theory seem incredible. The resurrection cannot be accounted for by a theory that Jesus simply revived after appearing to be dead.

Jesus died on the cross. The evidence is clear. The soldiers were sure of it. His enemies believed they were finished and done with him. His friends were cast into despair. As Luke said of Cleopas and another disciple, as they returned to their home after the crucifixion, "Their faces [were] full of gloom." Their conclusions about Jesus seemed tragic and irreversible: "But we had been hoping that he was the man to liberate Israel." (Luke 24:18-21, NEB) These people were not eagerly awaiting Jesus' resurrection from the dead (or recuperation from a drug). They believed death had had the final word on Jesus and all the bright hopes he had brought to their lives.

The Tomb and the Appearance

Two things started to become evident to both the friends and enemies of Jesus three days after his death. His tomb was empty, and some of his disciples had seen him alive.

The problem of the historian when he comes to the question of the empty tomb and the appearances of Jesus is much like the problem posed by the miracle stories. Both Christians and non-Christians of that day started with the fact of the empty tomb, just as they were forced to face Jesus' powers for healing. They differ on how they explain the way this thing came about. But there is no evidence that anyone at the time thought that Jesus was still in the same tomb in which he had been buried.

After all, how could Jesus' disciples have gone about preaching the resurrection of Christ, if they could be easily refuted by merely pointing out the grave in which his body lay? As one historian observed, the preaching of the resurrection "could not have been maintained in Jerusalem for a single day, for a single hour, if the emptiness of the tomb had not been established as a fact for all concerned." [2]

Jesus' opponents acted quickly to discount the empty tomb by claiming it was a fraud. The guards at Jesus' tomb were bribed to tell the people, "His disciples came by night and stole him away while we were asleep." (Matt. 28:13) This story was current already in the first century. It has been repeated many times since. Yet the opponents of Christianity could never produce the body, so eventually they started to tell people that the disciples had secretly reburied it. The one thing evident to anyone who wanted to deal with Jesus' resurrection was that his body was not in the tomb, nor could it be found.

The sheer fact of the empty tomb is not yet the full resurrection faith of the disciples. There is more to it than that. For example, the two disciples who were retreating in sadness to their homes in Emmaus knew of reports that Jesus' tomb was empty, yet they did not know that Jesus was raised from the dead. They reported that "some women of our company amazed us. They were at the tomb early in the morning and did not find his body. . . . Some of those who were with us went to the tomb, and found it just as the women had said. . . ." One crucial factor remained unfulfilled—"him they did not see." (Luke 24:22-24) The resurrection of Jesus is not simply that the tomb was empty but that Jesus had stepped back into the lives of his followers.

Reports of the appearance of Jesus to his disciples were also well known to both friend and foe alike. But again there were many explanations for those who did not want to face the implications for their own lives of Jesus' appearances.

Some attributed the appearances to the self-deception of the disciples, who could not abide the thought of being without their beloved teacher. Others implied more darkly that it was nothing but a plot on the part of the disciples to keep their present way of life as apostles and teachers alive. Faced with the grim necessity of going back to the dull work of fishing and farming, the critics of the new faith argued, the disciples set forth the notion of an empty tomb and the personal appearances of the dead Jesus to support their preaching. Such were the arguments of those who rejected faith in Jesus Christ to explain the empty tomb and the appearances. But the very creation of these arguments show the empty tomb and the appearances were basic facts that could not be pushed aside by either friend or foe.

For the person seeking the truth about Jesus, in the first century or the twentieth century, these facts remain. But what we have just called facts left Pilate and Herod and many others unconverted. What sense shall we make of them? Do they point to the central Christian affirmation: The Lord is risen indeed?

The Lord is Risen Indeed!

The initial reactions of the disciples to the reports of the empty tomb and the appearances of Jesus seem strange from the perspective of their later faith. When the women returned from the tomb to report to the disciples that Jesus was no longer there, "The story appeared to them to be nonsense, and they would not believe them." (Luke 24:11, NEB) Even when the disciples sent a party out to confirm the story and found it true, they still remained confused about its importance.

Along with disbelief, the other basic reaction was one of fear. After finding the tomb empty, the earliest witnesses "ran away from the tomb, beside themselves with terror." (Mark 16:8, NEB) They knew they were in the presence of an overwhelming mystery. The awe and mystery that surrounds death still lingered around this empty grave. They were quite unprepared for what had actually happened.

At the time of his death, the disciples had fled in confusion. Later they slowly huddled together in small groups, fearing what further vengence the enemies of Jesus would work on them. Perhaps they too would be the victims of the same powers that had put their Master to death.

Then an unexpected new fact broke upon them: Jesus was alive and was making his presence felt in their midst once more. There was in their new realization of his presence a sense of awe, but increasingly, as Jesus was personally encountered, the joy of his resurrection caught up his disciples. The crucial thing that started to happen to a few disciples, like those who went to the tomb and those on the road to Emmaus, eventually happened to more and more. They saw Jesus. Paul mentions a group of five hundred that saw him at one time. What was it that they saw? The New Testament uses one basic word to describe the resurrection appearances of Jesus: "body."

The word "body" in the New Testament means more than the physical framework in which we live. "Body" is a way of talking about the full reality of a person. The bodily resurrection of Jesus meant that the disciples did not conceive of Jesus' presence with them as simply his continuing moral influence, or just a particularly vivid and happy memory. They were experiencing the full reality of Jesus. He who had been with them was with them in a new and abiding way.

Yet this bodily-resurrected Jesus did not obey all those laws of physics that we believe bodies must obey. He disappeared from sight, only to appear later to people behind closed doors. His body was not bound by space and time, yet it had a reality that convinced the most doubting of his disciples, Thomas, that it was Jesus himself. This was clearly not the old mortal body of Jesus resuscitated to still mortal life. It was the body of Jesus transformed into a new kind of life.

Words fail us at this point. Paul invented a new one to express what had happened in the resurrection of Jesus. He called it a "spiritual body." Generally, we think of "spirit" and "body" as very different or even antagonistic realities. The New Testament writers did not view things that way, because for them "spiritual" did not mean a vague or half-real "something or other." The "spiritual" was that which had been transformed by and was controlled by the Holy Spirit. Before his death, Jesus was subject to physical limitations—he hungered, grew tired, finally died. After the resurrection he was free of all such limitations. Yet his spiritual body was not less real that the physical. It could even be said to be more real, for it was imperishable (1 Cor. 15:42-44).

The New Testament wants to make two things clear that we have difficulty believing belong together. It was really the total person of Jesus who was raised. At the same time, it is clear that the resurrection reality into which he had entered was not limited by space and time, by death and decay, as was his person before the resurrection. The resurrection of Jesus Christ was the coming into our world of a new kind of life, the eternal and abundant life of the kingdom of God. In his resurrection, Jesus Christ entered into the new life for which God has intended all human beings, the freedom of the kingdom of God.

The resurrection of Jesus also makes clear to disciples of all time a key dimension of the salvation that God has given through Christ. The empty tomb is the revelation of God's concern for every bit of human life. The salvation offered in Christ would be of a very different order if his body were still to be found in some unknown tomb in Palestine. We could say, in that case, that Jesus Christ is the savior of some small part of us, perhaps our souls or our minds. Instead, we say that through Jesus Christ we believe in the resurrection of the body. His redemption claims all aspects of our lives, our total beings. The Bible sees humankind as a body-soul combination. God's work of redemption is not complete until the bodies are raised, first that of Jesus, and some day those of all believers.

Discerning His Presence

The question is, how do we become aware of the presence of the risen Christ? Many ways are evident in the earliest witnesses of the disciples. Some met the risen Christ in Christian preaching and teaching. As the two disciples from Emmaus recalled how Christ had expounded Scripture to them, they said, "Did not our hearts burn within us . . . while he opened to us the scriptures?" (Luke 24:32) Again and again it has happened that people perceive and respond to the risen Christ when he is proclaimed through the use of the Scriptures.

> We look at the records of an Event—an odd Event with some logically odd edges to it—and because we have read the gospels and wondered who this person is of whom this Event is narrated, we are forced to ask theological questions of it. For

some people—not for all . . .—the moment of disclosure comes. It does not come by straightforward inference from the events narrated, nor by logical deduction. . . . But some people read of the resurrection and are able to say, "*My* Lord and *my* God." [3]

Christ may be discerned when the Scriptures are faithfully taught, for, in the Spirit, our words become his words. But there has to be an openness and expectancy on the part of those who listen. Listening is not a passive business of having information poured into you. Listening means the responsibility of being open to what is being said. Just as during his earthly ministry, so now in his continuing ministry as risen Lord, Jesus says, "Having eyes do you not see, and having ears do you not hear?" (Mark 8:18)

Disciples in every age have found that participating in the Lord's Supper became an opportunity for encountering the risen Christ. This was shown already on the first Easter when Cleopas and another disciple had their eyes opened to the presence of Jesus as he broke bread with them. "He was known to them in the breaking of the bread." (Luke 24:35) The breaking of bread and the sharing of the wine are the means of knowing the presence of the risen one and of being strengthened by him. The significance of the meal comes not from any special virtue in the physical elements, nor from the holiness of the participants. It comes from the reality of Jesus Christ himself who is present. He is the one who feeds us in spiritual ways. Having met him in the communion, Christians found something else. Be it around a family table or in a church basement or along the side of the road, in any meal where bread is broken and shared in his name, Jesus the Lord is made known.

There are other ways. In the gathering of Christians to share with one another what God has done for them, to sing his praises, and to celebrate their sharing in the gospel, the risen Lord can be known. It may be another person who can open your eyes to the reality of Jesus Christ. It may be in an act of service to others that you discern him—in a child who has been given a carton of milk, or while delivering "meals on wheels" to an elderly shut-in. Or it can be in a silent moment of openness that his presence becomes clear.

Because he is Lord, he is free to confront people in unexpected ways. This is what happened to Paul on the road to Damascus (Acts 9). It has happened to others. Yet the sudden and dramatic confrontation with Christ that some experience does not mean those who have recognized and acknowledged him more slowly do not really know him. Whether one feels his presence in a moment of dramatic insight or grows gradually to an ever fuller awareness of it, it is the risen Christ who makes it possible to become a disciple at all.

Our Response

The resurrection of Jesus established a new possibility for humanity. Now people may share in new life beacuse Jesus is their contemporary. To say this new life is a possibility for everyone does not mean it has become real to everyone. The risen Christ now, as during his earthly ministry, calls for a response. This response is described by two words: repentance and faith.

Repentance goes deeper than an emotion of the moment. To repent is not only to recognize your inability to overcome that sin. Repentance is an about-face in which you turn from being preoccupied with yourself and become open to another person. This other person is Jesus Christ, present in this risen power.

Responding to Jesus Christ grows out of turning loose all attempts to reshape ourselves and our world. The problem of the Pharisees, Zealots, and Essenes, both ancient and modern, is their unwillingness to give up their own attempts at salvation. They think they already know how the world is to be saved. They only want Jesus as they can fit him into their scheme for salvation. Jesus will have no part of this. We can never know him as long as we try to make Jesus a part of our own plan for saving the world or ourselves. To do so is to be unrepentant. The disciple is willing to break with his whole past, even his self-created claims to goodness, hope, and joy, to receive the Christ.

Faith is the other basic word for our response to Jesus Christ. When in repentance we are open to his presence, faith becomes a possibility. Faith is personal trust that brings us into a relationship with Jesus Christ. The words we use to express our faith in Jesus Christ do not create our relationship to him. It is the relationship with Jesus that gives the doctrines, creeds, and confessions their real meaning. Christian faith is not a kind of stubborn belief in spite of the evidence. It is being open and accepting to a new kind of evidence—the presence of the risen Jesus in the world today.

One of the more spectacular professions of such a response in recent years has been that of former White House aide Charles Colson. Note in this editorial the references both to the repentance and to the faith in the risen Christ that we have been describing.

> Before his recent conversion, Charles Colson had a reputation in Washington as being just about the meanest man in town. . . .
>
> Which is why his sudden embrace of Christianity has left many people a bit unsettled. At the Federal Courthouse in Washington, after being sentenced to a one-to-three-year prison term for obstructing justice in the Ellsberg case, Mr. Colson greeted television and print media reporters with the simple declaration: "I've committed my life to Jesus Christ." . . .
>
> By his own testimony, he is a new man "in Christ." This means quite simply that he is starting over again, viewing the world from a completely different perspective from the one he had as a White House hatchet man. . . . He has said he has been converted, and until his behavior proved otherwise, he is entitled to be believed. . . .
>
> There is a freshness in his announcement, for it comes from a man who, by his own admission, had not known Christ until this point in his life. To many Christians the use of religious language in public sounds a bit strange because we seldom have need to preface our involvement in daily decisions with the presupposition that our life is guided by a commitment to Christ. We should not, however, be disturbed over Mr. Colson's use of the term; it is an exciting event to be well into adulthood before finding the freedom and joy of a conversion to Christ. . . .
>
> Perhaps our secular friends would better understand the way we view Mr. Colson's newfound faith if they would realize that as a statement of faith, what he has just announced is comparable to his having made an announcement in 1972 that "my first commitment is to myself and to my utilization of political power"—which, of course, he didn't do, for such candor is not the style in the moral universe Mr. Colson occupied in 1972. Everything he has done since he entered the White House testifies to his preconversion commitment. Today he has a new commitment. It has transformed his life and has opened

the way for him to apply his intellect to the complex issues of secular society from a new perspective. Let others ponder whether Mr. Colson's conversion is authentic or not. What matters is that one who was lost now testifies that he has been found. We rejoice with Mr. Colson in his new beginning.[4]

6 | God Getting Next to Us

We have met the charismatic or Spirit-gifted Jesus who drew and draws disciples to himself as they choose his way to face life instead of the way of tradition, of revolution, or of retreat. We have discovered him to be the crucified Jesus who calls on us to die to the old patterns of living, and we have seen in the risen Christ the secret of new and transformed life for those who will repent and believe the good news. It would seem that there is little more to say. However, before we go on to look at Jesus' impact on certain crucial areas of contemporary life, one more point must be made, a point so important that it really is the climax of this section.

Human and Divine

Jesus was a true human being. Indeed, he was more fully human than we are because he was free of self-centeredness, pride, fear, and dishonesty. He lived without being distorted into sin by the threats and anxieties of life. Jesus was "one who has been tempted in every way that we are, though he is without sin." (Heb. 4:15, JB) Yet having said all this about Jesus, the earliest Christians went on to say, "God was in Christ." (2 Cor. 5:19) They were insisting that the importance of Jesus surpasses his humanness. In him we meet the eternal God.

Christians have tried to express this illogical, paradoxical faith in many ways. Some ways have proved helpful to some people, while others seem only to add to our confusion.

For instance, the early church spoke, in one of its confessions, of Jesus Christ's being of "two natures in one person." There is the divine nature and human nature in Jesus. These natures had come together to form one single, fully integrated person. Thus Jesus is both God and man.

This way of thinking about how God was in Christ has been very helpful to many, yet it is an idea that is hard to visualize. The picture that comes to my mind inevitably is that of the old-fashioned milk bottle. In the days of old, before homogenized milk —this illustration is really not for those under forty—the cream inevitably rose to the top of a milk bottle. High quality milk came with a thick layer of golden cream. The cheaper milk, which usually made its way to the poorer homes in town, had only the slimmest layer of cream floating on top of a bottle of thin, pale milk. In either case, as the cream increased, the skim milk decreased, and vice versa.

Some popular views of Christ follow the milk bottle analogy. There are those who emphasize the divinity of Christ, like the cream in the old-fashioned milk bottle. For them, as the divinity increases, the humanity decreases. In asserting clearly that it is *God* who is in Christ, the involvement of Jesus in the common lot of humanity is lessened and lessened, sometimes almost to the disappearing point. The divine nature of Christ is affirmed at the expense of his human nature.

On the other hand, some want to see Jesus solely in terms of his human nature. The picture painted is that of the human Jesus, uniquely open to his neighbors and to the creative forces of love in the universe. His humanity is total, while his divinity has been reduced to that of being "one deeply inspired by God" or one who "recognizes the spark of divinity that is in everyone." The reality of his humanity has been assured, but at the price of his real divinity.

Thankfully, Jesus Christ lives beyond the false alternatives given to us by the all-too-popular "milk bottle" approach. In fact, the very people who first used the term "two natures in one person" went on to speak of Jesus Christ as being *both* fully human and fully divine. Deity and humanity are both authentically present in Jesus Christ, and they do not cancel one another out. I suppose homogenized milk would be suggested, with both cream and skim milk, deity and humanity, present and inseparable throughout.

But we had best cast aside outmoded milk bottles and try some new ways of confessing faith in Jesus Christ. A better analogy to the freeing needed by the mind to get in tune with Christ is found in the kind of shock one feels in trying to cope with education's new math.

A child comes home from school babbling with excitement about "sets" or "changing number bases" or "theorems of transformation" to parents who had trouble with the old math of twenty or thirty years before. What is apparent is that the children are moving with ease through a world of thought utterly alien to our own. It is a world that admits as possible things that seem downright impossible to us.

The same thing is happening in other areas, and unless people are willing to accept their obsolescence with grace, they had best get ready to have their minds opened in a radical way—to have their minds "blown," is the way modern slang puts it.

This is just what happened centuries ago with the coming of Jesus Christ. It is something that is happening even now when a person accepts Jesus Christ personally. People come in touch with a reality in Jesus Christ that transforms their usual ways of thinking and believing. As you enter the new reality given in Christ, you have to be ready to think in new ways about him. Let's try to penetrate the meaning of some of the basic ways in which Christ has been confessed as "God with us," the unique divine-human being. We'll start with efforts to interpret his deity.

God Was in Christ

The Bible speaks frequently of the way God was in Christ in terms of the relationship of parent to child. "Jesus Christ is the Son of God" is a formula found in every corner of Christian thought and life. This gives us some intimation of what it means to say that he is divine, for we know in how many ways children are like parents. Parents, for instance, may hope their children will escape the nearsightedness and baldness that has plagued the family for generations, yet such hopes are often frustrated. "Like father, like son," we say.

Son of God

But our human experience gives us only a beginning notion of what it means to confess Jesus Christ as the Son of God. There is a relationship between Jesus and God that exists between no human parent and child. The reason is simply stated in the words of Jesus in the Gospel of John: "I and the Father are one." (John 10:30) Looked at from the perspective of our faith, this means that when we know Christ, we know his Father also. In Jesus we do not encounter a descendant of God who may be only a pale reflection of him. Rather, to use our modern slogan, he is "the real thing." Jesus is the Son of God, but he is also one with God.

However, Christians have never been satisfied with any one term to describe what God has done through Jesus Christ. The beginning of the Gospel of John speaks of Jesus Christ as the Word made flesh. Again our ordinary, human thoughts will carry us only part of the way toward seeing just what this tells us about Jesus. But even that partial illumination may help us on the road of faith.

Word of God

Many of our words are flippant and well forgotten. Yet there are some words we speak that are deep and serious, that bear our deepest feelings and express our ultimate commitments. Words of love are an example. Such words are a kind of extension of ourselves, the direct, immediate expression of the real self. When a man and woman say to one another, "Yes, I do love you and will marry you," their words are not empty verbalisms. They have given themselves to one another.

It was out of this sense of the importance of words that the Gospel of John was able to speak of Jesus Christ as the eternal, creative Word spoken by God. "When all things began, the Word already was. The Word dwelt with God, and what God was, the Word was." (John 1:1, NEB) The Word God speaks to us in Jesus is not simply more information about God or yet another set of rules for life. It is life itself, because God is in that Word in such a way that "what God was, the Word was." There is in Jesus Christ the power and reality of God. And now we can know and live by that Word because, in the coming of Jesus, "the Word became flesh." (John 1:14)

Human experience can give us some intimation of what is

meant by "the Word became flesh." A child is born to a couple whose words of love have bound them to one another. Their words of love have become flesh in and through their child. The brave words of commitment spoken by the people undertaking an anti-hunger program become flesh in the money or the meal they share with the hungry. The mother's words of love for her child become flesh in the embrace that picks up the victim of the skinned knee. Our human words are constantly seeking to be made flesh in acts that make this world a bit more human.

Yet as long as these words are the words of weak and sinful people, they will never completely be made flesh. Our commitments and intentions will falter and fail. The Word that God has spoken in Christ does not fail, nor is its expression in flesh broken and imperfect. "And the Word became flesh and dwelt among us, full of grace and truth; we have beheld his glory, glory as of the only Son from the Father." (John 1:14)

Karl Barth, a great teacher of the church in our own century, said that in Jesus Christ, God "assumed His likeness to us, and that now He is to be sought and found of us here, namely, in His human being." [5] Jesus is not simply a ray of bright light sent into our darkness; the power of the sun itself is found in him. Jesus Christ is not only the stream that brings us water; he is the spring from which the water comes. He is not only the slender cable that brings transforming power to our weakness; he is the dynamo that produces the power itself.

Christians keep talking about this mysterious, hard-to-explain reality they encounter in Jesus Christ because they know it to be the source of salvation. It is always easy to condemn the unbending insistence of some Christians that the divinity of Christ must be confessed in just a certain way. It is wise to avoid their rigidities, yet it is very unwise to forget the seriousness and passion with which they speak of Jesus Christ. To speak of Jesus accurately is crucial because we are dealing with matters of life and death. To confess that "God was in Christ" is vital, because through him God was "reconciling the world to himself." The confession of Jesus Christ is acknowledging the divine source of our salvation and hope. In Jesus, God was getting next to us as never before or since in human history.

"And Was Made Man"

Christians have also been intent on insisting that Jesus was a real human being. The union between God and humankind took place in one particular person, Jesus of Nazareth.

It has always been easy to see how God could have entered in what we like to call "the higher" or "spiritual" aspects of human nature, the mind or spirit. But how about the other parts of our nature? Does God have anything to do with them?

The New Testament is quite clear on this point. "The Word became flesh." God became identified with all that we are, not only our minds or spirits but also our bodies with their appetites and desires and frailties. To forget this is to bypass the real meaning of what happened in Jesus Christ.

This is the mystery which we celebrate at Christmas. Some early Christians summed it up in the confessional statement issued at Nicea in A.D. 351, when the church was trying to find some common statement of belief. They described Jesus as the one "who for us men, and for our salvation, came down from heaven, and was incarnate by the Holy Spirit of the Virgin Mary, and was made man. . . ." What does it really mean to say that in Jesus Christ, God "was made man"? This is a difficult question that forces us to think about just what it is that makes up our humanness.

Certain things are evident when we first start to think about the question of Jesus' humanity. The Gospels make it plain that he lived with a body just like ours. He got hungry and thirsty, he grew tired and had to sleep. As evident as this all may seem to us today, there have been people that doubted that Jesus could ever have been involved in a physical existence like our own. In a well meaning but misguided effort to compliment Jesus, they started to say all sorts of silly things. Jesus, they said, did not really get hungry or thirsty or need rest or sleep. He just did these things to keep from embarrassing his disciples who had not yet reached his level of perfection. They wanted to insist that Jesus was all mind, or spirit, that he did not have a truly physical body.

Whenever people start thinking this way, they are not so much glorifying the divinity of Christ as they are despising their own bodies. To reject the reality of Jesus' physical life is to treat human bodies as if they were too unclean for God to have anything to do with them. The reality of Jesus Christ points in just the opposite direction. This is consistent with the Biblical view of humanity to which we referred in the last chapter. We are not souls temporarily living in physical bodies; we are a body-soul combination. God's plan of redemption involves our bodies too.

The incarnation also makes it clear that God is committed to full bellies, strong bones, and clear vision. God was in Christ for the healing not only of troubled spirits and sinful wills but of hurting and hungry bodies as well. If we go wrong at this point in our confession of Christ, we miss out on one whole side of what God is doing in our world.

Let's see if we can take the humanity of Christ seriously at still a deeper level than the physical. What can we say about Jesus' mental and spiritual life? It was truly human. Jesus was wise, but there were things he did not know. He had to grow in knowledge just as he did in bodily stature. Hence we may assume that he, like the other boys of Nazareth, attended a synagogue school and memorized Scripture and rabbinic teaching, though the details of his boyhood years remain hidden from us.

The only incident that is found in the Gospels, the story of his visit to the Temple in Jerusalem, underscores his unique relationship to God ("your father and I have been looking for you". . . . "I must be in my Father's house" [Luke 2:48-49]), but it also makes clear his humanness. In his eagerness to pursue his interests, Jesus acted not unlike other eager young people to this day. He went after his goal of talking with the learned teachers with such zeal that he forgot to tell his parents of his whereabouts. When this was called to his attention by his worried mother, he responded with the open-faced wonder of those so intent on their goal as to forget those around them.

It was one of those incidents which modern parents usually conclude by saying, "Son, there must have been a breakdown of communication between us." Joseph or Mary would never put it that way. They were up against the wonderful, but at times vexing, reality of a vitally alive young person forging eagerly ahead to maturity. Yet Jesus went back to Nazareth to be obedient to them. Luke summed it all up in one sentence: "And Jesus grew up, both in body and in wisdom, gaining favor with God and men." (Luke 2:52, TEV)

Not only was Jesus a human being; he lived at a particular time and place in history. He was a Jew of first century Palestine. He attended synagogue and worshiped in the great Temple of Jerusalem. He learned his prayers from his parents and teachers as did the other boys in his village. While from various motives Christianity often has tried to brush these facts aside, Jesus' life and piety were shaped by Judaism. His prayer life, and the great prayers he gave his disciples, bear the stamp of Jewish piety. His teachings were clearly shaped by the great Jewish writers, for many of them parallel the Jewish collection of writings called the Talmud. When Jesus was asked which was the greatest commandment, he replied with the great fundamental text of Judaism, the *Shema Israel* (Deut. 6:5), adding to it a part of Leviticus 19:18: " 'Hear, O Israel: The Lord our God, the Lord is one; and you shall love the Lord your God with all your heart, and with all your soul, and with all your mind, and with all your strength.' The second is this, 'You shall love your neighbor as yourself.' There is no other commandment greater than these." (Mark 12:29-31)

The Struggles of the Inner Life

There is still another level of questions that needs to be dealt with in finding the full measure of Jesus' humanity. These are the questions about his moral and spiritual life. There is a kind of piety that finds it difficult to even envisage questions about Jesus' religious life or his struggle with ethical decisions. If he is truly God incarnate, we like to think, how could there be any possible struggle or agony in his inner life?

Yet the New Testament makes it abundantly clear that he prayed deeply and passionately to find his Father's will, as when he spent a whole night in prayer before choosing the Twelve (Luke 6:12-16). Jesus' communion with God the Father in prayer was profound, reaching to a depth surely untouched in our shallow attempts at praying. Yet in the deepest crisis of his life, he felt himself forgotten by God. On the cross, he cried out, "My God, my God, why hast thou forsaken me?" Jesus knew about the joy of close fellowship with God. He knew also the dreadful experience of feeling forgotten by God. In all this, he was giving reality to his identity with us as truly human.

In the Letter to the Hebrews, the question of Jesus' true identity with humankind is pushed to its most extreme point. In showing how Jesus as the Son of God was prepared for his task of acting as the great high priest who could finally deal with human sin, the author wrote, "For it is not as if we had a high priest who was incapable of feeling our weaknesses with us; but we have one who has been tempted in every way that we are, though he is without sin." (Heb. 4:15, JB)

The difficulty we have in dealing with this approach to Jesus' humanity is with that word *temptation*. We tend to equate temptation with sin. This is natural for most of us, because we are all too easily disposed to follow Oscar Wilde's cynical advice, "The only way to get rid of a temptation is to yield to it." But temptation is not sin. To recognize as attractive the possibility of evil and then not to do the evil is temptation but not sin. To say that Jesus "has been tempted in every way that we are" does not mean he sinned, but it does mean he might have. We discussed earlier (pp. 40-41) his temptation to misuse his charisma, his power and influence over others, a temptation clearly described in the Gospels. But Hebrews 4:15 surely suggests that he also knew the lure of many other kinds of evil, including sexual temptation, since he was truly man.

In saying all this about Jesus, we are saying that he shared in the way God created all humans. There is one vital difference from us. Jesus did not misuse his powers. He did not pervert his freedom. Having been tempted, he is able to "sympathize with our weaknesses," but he does so "without sinning." (Heb 4:15, RSV)

To confess the humanity of Jesus means that he knew not only the severity of life but also its joys. He did not believe in the kind of self-denial that frowns on a good meal or a convivial evening with friends. Jesus himself made this clear when people apparently complained that he didn't resemble John the Baptist in his life-style. Jesus knew that they were trying to catch him. You perhaps know the game yourself—people sometimes play it on their new ministers. Someone says, "Isn't it too bad Rev. Whomsoever doesn't do it like dear old Dr. Whatsoever did?" Now Jesus was not interested in becoming the victim of their game, so he spread the record out for all to see. "For John came neither eating and drinking, and they say, 'He has a demon'; the Son of man came eating and drinking, and they say, 'Behold, a glutton and a drunkard, a friend of tax collectors and sinners!' " (Matt. 11:18-19)

To the great annoyance of many, Jesus enjoyed meals with those considered to be sinners and outcasts, like Zaccheus (Luke 19:1-10) or Matthew (Matt. 9:9-13). We have a Savior who could enjoy God's creation. To confess the true humanness of Jesus means he is one with us not only in our trials and temptations but also in our joys and victories. His humanity places him next to us not only at the communion table in its solemnity but in the midst of the laughing teenagers in the pizza parlor or in the fun of a wedding reception.

Does This Make You Feel Uneasy?

Thinking about Jesus in this way has always tended to make uneasy many who believe in him as the Christ, as God incarnate. If he were all this human, how could he still really be divine? They feel more comfortable religiously with another picture of Jesus. He looks like a human being, but somehow he hovers just above the plane of real humanity. In one of the eastern religious traditions, the savior-god who comes to earth is pictured as someone who walks ever so slightly above the ground. To most people his identity remains unknown. To the perceptive, the mystery is evident. The clue is that a god-come-to-earth never sweats or gets dirt on his feet, no matter how hot the day or dusty the road.

For us the real good news is that our faith is in a Savior who got his feet dirty. The final gap between God and his creatures has been closed in Jesus Christ. Because the gap has been closed, men and women can start to live a life transformed by God.

We must always be wary of a piety that likes to preserve the divinity of Jesus by picturing him in a robe that always looks like the "after" of a detergent ad, or with hair that is never ruffled. This is not the real Jesus. The real mystery of the Word become flesh is that in Jesus, a real man, God himself is present. Jesus Christ is good news because through him God is involved totally with us as human beings. He has stooped to our lowest lowliness. Paul, probably quoting an early Christian hymn, speaks thus of Jesus: "His state was divine, yet he did not cling to his equality with God but emptied himself to assume the condition of a slave, and became as men are; and being as all men are, he was humbler yet, even to accepting death, death on a cross." (Phil. 2:6-8, JB)

Words of Personal Meaning

Having looked at some of the basic ways in which disciples of Jesus have made their confession of him as Lord, you may have wondered how you could ever make these confessions real in your own life. Christians have been saying and singing these kinds of words about Jesus for generations—they certainly have the sanctity of tradition behind them. But answering the fundamental questions of Christian thought and life in other people's words leaves most of us dissatisfied. We need a link between the great fundamentals of the faith and our own personal life of faith.

This sense of remoteness about the traditional affirmations of Christ is not a particularly new problem, nor is it a sign of unbelief. It simply reflects the fact that the ways we express our faith and share our deepest feelings change. The language of love of the twentieth century is different from that of the nineteenth, and most certainly different from that of the first century. But the power and reality of love has always been the bond holding the human family together.

Similarly the language of faith changes. We need to find what Jesus' power and presence mean in relation to *our* questions and needs. We must always be careful to go back to the witness of the Scripture to Jesus Christ to find an authentic word to speak about him. But we need a new kind of boldness in translating Scripture into those very personal and contemporary words that answer the questions we ask now. This is a kind of task in which all of us are involved. Perhaps you will be willing to try it, if you start to see what others have been doing.

Three elements have always gone into finding new ways to

confess Jesus Christ. The first is the reality in every time and place of his power and love as risen Lord. We are not creating his presence and power by our words—we are disclosing that he has been there all along. The second element is the witness of the Bible to his power and meaning. Finally, there are the questions and needs and problems we bring to our search for the real Jesus.

One way we can define our personal understanding of Jesus is to draw on words or slogans that we use every day. Perhaps a look at what other people have used can free you to try some of your own.

From the realm of government people have taken the word "king" to confess the power of Jesus—he is the ruler of life. From the language of the slave market they have taken the word "redeemer"—the one who pays the price for setting the slave free—to characterize his liberating power. From ancient medicine comes the word "savior"—the healer who brings wholeness and life to men and women. These are some of the great terms with universal appeal.

Other terms have had only limited or local appeal in their work of witness. For example, back in the seventeenth century a man called Stephen Nye was carried away with the importance of military terms. He described Jesus with the unexpected phrase, "God's Lieutenant." To explain Jesus' power he wanted to use a word that was near at hand and understood by the people to whom he was speaking. So, he said, Jesus Christ is the one "whom the Father hath made his Lieutenant. . . ." Jesus is the line officer giving orders to the troops and joining them in the struggle against evil being directed by God.

How would you go about formulating your own witness about who Jesus is and what he has done for you, to share with those amid whom you live and work? Do your attempts reflect the "mind-blowing" truth that Jesus Christ is both divine and human?

7 | Jesus and Human Liberation

Jesus' disciples in Palestine quickly discovered that the power and presence of Jesus enfolded all of life, so that the old and easily assumed ways of living and thinking were being changed. We who have followed them in later centuries have had the same experience, and this study would not be complete unless we consider the impact of Jesus Christ on today's world as well as on the individual. So we go on by looking at four areas of contemporary importance that Jesus enables his disciples to approach in a new spirit.

Nowhere is this seen more vividly today than in the growing awareness of the real significance of two of the phrases Jesus quoted early in his ministry: "The Spirit of the Lord . . . has sent me to proclaim release to the captives, . . . to set at liberty those who are oppressed. . . ." (Luke 4:18) Jesus has let loose a power of liberation that could change all that we have assumed about people's "rightful place" in the world! It was this power of liberation that Paul was reflecting on when he said, "For as many of you as were baptized into Christ have put on Christ. There is neither Jew nor Greek, there is neither slave nor free, there is neither male nor female, for you are all one in Christ Jesus." (Gal. 3:27-28)

The disciples found that the power of the risen Lord was beginning to break down all of the neat little distinctions by which people had tried to get special privileges for themselves. We are aware of this today. But the thing we keep discovering afresh is just how imperfectly we have expressed this radical new oneness in Christ. It is most disturbing to see how we fall short of the freedom in Christ because deliberately or unconsciously we cling to those old ways that leave the world divided between the oppressors and the oppressed.

So the work of liberation to oneness in Christ that started almost two thousand years ago has become a fresh order of the day for twentieth century disciples. Sad to say, we are still confronted by tension between Jews and Gentiles, between enslaved peoples and their masters, and, in a new way, between male and female. Anti-semitism can still be found in neighborhoods and churches, though it is more often whispered than shouted. Such bitter fruits of slavery as racism still flourish in human hearts, even if slavery itself is no longer on the law books. And at no point has the modern liberation movement touched a more tender nerve than when it comes to women's liberation. Liberation continues to be an issue, and disciples must face it in new and radical ways in our time.

Let's see if we can get some perspective on modern movements for liberation. Something started with the coming of Jesus Christ of which the world has not heard the end; in fact, his work will not be completed until the kingdom of God rules. Jesus Christ is calling the whole world and every aspect of its life to new being in and through himself. A major goal is liberation, in which men and women are to be set free from all the oppressions that divide us, as we are to be free from all the other bondage that sin has created.

Presently, we are in the situation like that of the conquered peoples of Europe who were under Nazi domination during World War II. With the landing of the Allies on Normandy beaches on D-Day, 1944, their liberation was at hand. The decisive battle had been fought. Yet there were still many dangerous and difficult times ahead, and the forces of liberation still had much to do. In fact, one of the problems was that many of the conquered peoples did not yet grasp the fact that the liberating forces had been let loose in their midst. They had no consciousness of liberation. They kept on living as if the old forces of oppression would prevail forever.

In much the same way, the liberation of men and women in Christ started with his life, death, and resurrection. Although the decisive battle has been won, the "mopping up" operation still goes on, for there is much oppression. In these battles the crucial question is whether people are conscious of the liberating power loose in the world and will work with it, or whether they still believe the old forces of oppression will rule the future.

Jesus and Slavery

We can see in history how slowly liberation often is effected. Look, for example, at a division in society that for thousands of years people simply took for granted, the division between free people and slaves. We have seen that new life in Christ means that ". . . there is neither slave nor free, . . . for you are all one in Christ Jesus." (Gal. 3:28) This liberating force had been let loose in Christ's coming, but it took centuries before its full meaning was to break upon humankind. Instead, arguments were formulated by the owners of slaves, including many pious Christians, to show that slavery was God's will and a good thing. Owners always found these arguments convincing, even if the slaves did not. The deeper tragedy, however, was that they did get many of the slaves to accept their owners' view. They accepted the inferiority claimed by their owners' characterization. Worse than their chains was this denial of a full consciousness of their true worth as children of God created for freedom in Christ.

Then, slowly, a new consciousness started to dawn on people. In the United States, slaves like Nat Turner and Harriet Tubman caught the vision of a destiny for slaves as truly free people. An increasing number of Southerners who had reaped the benefits of slavery came through faith in Jesus Christ to see the evil in it and worked for its abolition. Tragically, it took a war to accomplish it, but eventually slavery as an institution was torn down. Today it is inconceivable that it would ever be restored, for in this area of life most people have grasped the meaning of the liberation offered by Christ. The shackles of slavery did not fall in this country until the end of the Civil War, but the decisive battle had been fought by Jesus Christ nearly two thousand years before.

Now in the United States the struggle for full liberation in Christ still goes on, but it has moved deeper into the territory of human bondage. With the civil rights legislation of recent years the legal vestiges of slavery were crushed. What we are involved in today is a struggle against the deeper, inner slavery of warped attitudes and self-hate. And as was foreseen by one of the great liberators in Jesus' power, the late Martin Luther King, Jr., the search for this freedom may be even more painful than the legislative struggle, but here, too, eventual victory is sure.

"Consciousness Raising"

God's work of liberation of people gets its start in our lives when we become conscious of our need and of the possibility of being free; the story of slavery and civil rights illustrates this. Hence many of the modern liberation movements speak of "consciousness raising." Every great movement of liberation has had at its start a small group of people who have fired in the imagination (or consciousness) of others the dream of freedom.

Early Christian preaching had this effect on people. They were the victims of personal sinfulness and guilt, of oppressive religious systems, and of exploitive governments. They had been this way for so long that they were almost numbed into believing that this was just the way it had to be. Then the good news about Jesus Christ brought them the possibility of being lifted into a new kind of freedom, and they responded to him in repentance and faith. Slaves did not lose their chains immediately, but even they found new dignity and worth as the freed people of the Lord (1 Cor. 7:22).

The founders of the United States dreamed of a state where religious liberty and human dignity were respected. The anti-slavery forces dreamed of a time when all could be free, and by daring to dream they opened the way for this possibility. In our own time, people are dreaming bold dreams of how men and women may be liberated from all sorts of oppression and want, and this God-given restlessness is inspiring the search for new paths to freedom.

When we talk of liberation, furthermore, we are not just talking about "them." God's work of liberation is all of a piece. It is not that those of us in the church are fully liberated and must now liberate other people. Rather, we are all in the process of being freed from various forms of bondage. What white Christian over 35 has not in the past 20 years come, however reluctantly, to a new awareness of the oppression black people have endured in this "free land"? Twenty years from now, what new insights will God have led us to

gain? We cannot talk of liberation and of sharing the freeing love
of God with others in a kind of paternalistic way, as if we only give
to others who are in need. Rather, to paraphrase D. T. Niles'
definition of evangelism, we are one slave telling another slave where
freedom is to be found.

This is important to remember because, when "consciousness
raising" takes place, its impact soon starts to be felt—an impact
which can be upsetting. Change in ourselves does not come easy
to most of us. Furthermore, when others seek liberation it almost
inevitably seems threatening. For instance, right now, in many of
our churches and communities and homes, we are feeling, sometimes
painfully, the effect of the search for economic and political liberation
of many other peoples. The poor and oppressed of our inner city
ghettos, the American Indians, the disadvantaged farm or migrant
worker, the peasants and workers of Latin American countries and
African nations—all these and others have moved slowly from apathy
and resignation to a new consciousness or awareness, to the restless
search for action.

For those of us that sit on the side of so much political privilege
and economic affluence, all this can seem terribly threatening.
Perhaps we find ourselves in this situation: we once spoke confidently
of brave new worlds that were to emerge through social and political
and economic liberation. But now we find ourselves and our futures
seemingly threatened by demands and movements that we did not
guess would come into existence, and we are tempted to forsake our
commitments to liberation. Our Christian hope for a more just
world through the power of Christ has been shaken and threatened
in very basic ways. The chaos of our inner cities, the growing
economic disorder, and our fears for the future combine to undercut
the wavering faith we have had in liberation as God's work. How
are we to view it? How should we respond?

That liberation from sin and evil is God's work was made clear
by Jesus in Nazareth (Luke 4) and at Calvary. Our earlier illustration (p. 80) about the liberation of Europe during World War II
perhaps can help us understand the significance of the events of the
present. No matter what bold step was taken towards the liberation,
there were still many difficult battles left to fight. While in the midst

of those wartime struggles, people were often tempted to fear that the future of liberation was not certain.

We, too, are in the midst of a struggle, and the way to liberation is hard. But at a time when Christians are tempted to abandon our concern for the liberation of the oppressed or to cease sharing our resources with the needy, we must ask ourselves a question: Where is faithfulness to Christ in his work of liberation needed, and what is its price?

As the work of liberation leads us through difficult places, we are tempted to run back to the old imagined certainties of the past. We may even make Martin Luther King into a kind of Protestant saint but ignore the work of liberation to which he gave his life. Rather, we had best ask ourselves, what is it that God is doing in the work of liberation in our community, in our midst at this time, and where do we stand in relationship to this work?

Who Near You Looks For Liberation?

Some strivings for liberation are going on right now in your own community and your own church of which you may be only vaguely aware. For example, we are in the midst of a time of consciousness raising about the needs of the older people of our world.

There is a growing outcry from the older members of our communities not only for adequate physical existence, but also for lives filled with some meaning, hope, and love. They are looking for freedom from the oppression of indifference and of being walled-off in homes and institutions that isolate them from life and from us. They are rising up to remind us that a social security check provides a meager way of life in the midst of an economy like ours, and that so often the old-age hospital, the mental institution, or the dreary isolation of a ghetto apartment are utterly inadequate places for finding a dignified and meaningful old age.

So here we are confronted by those who have a vision of life that comes from Christian faith. They ask us what we will do in allowing them to live life abundantly through all of their days. The exploitation and ignoring of the aged is a need that cries out for liberation. It is one to which many churches have sought to respond.

It is the witness to one of the ways in which Jesus and his disciples are moving in our time and generation.

There are other movements of liberation. The physically and mentally handicapped are struggling to find the freedom to live and work up to their own abilities instead of being pushed to the sidelines of our society. Children need to be liberated from brutalizing institutions to which they are sent when they come into conflict with the adult world, or from educational patterns that tend to stifle their natural desire to learn rather than to encourage it. How about the youth in your congregation? Are they free to participate fully, or are they still second-class members? To find the beginning point for a liberation movement we need not go to some distant place. We can find such stirrings in our own communities, perhaps even in our own hearts.

Women's Liberation

There is another kind of liberation stirring in our midst. The clear and persistent demands of women for equality and justice have stirred every aspect of life, and none more deeply than the church and the family. But aren't churches already a preserve of women? Yes, say the liberation groups, but please note carefully that women are usually in the children's classroom, the kitchen, or the choir; a few are on the official boards; almost never is one in the pulpit. The officers often welcome an ordained woman to do Christian education, but even to consider one as *the pastor* sends tremors of tension through almost any congregation.

Jesus lived in a society where the place of women was clearly and, people assumed, permanently set. Jewish life, like that of most societies in the ancient world, was patriarchal. "Papa knows best" was not a half-joking quip, as it can be with us, but a serious belief around which life was shaped. Women's functions were those of wife and mother. While in the Bible there were glorious exceptions like Miriam and Esther who could become national heroines, most women lived under serious legal disabilities and limitations. There was real appreciation for feminine beauty and the wonder of sexual love in the Song of Solomon, and admiration for a woman's intelligence, industry, and piety is voiced in the Book of Proverbs. But men were also warned about the dangers of women, who were pictured as often contentious, noisy, indiscreet, and the source of temptation (as in Prov. 9:13; 11:22; 25:24). Men might be willing to grant women salvation in the world to come, but they intended to keep a strong hand on them in this world. The liberation that comes from faith in God was extended in only a limited way to women in Old Testament times.

Many women appear in the Gospels and the stories of the early church. Some we know by name, like Mary Magdalene, Mary the mother of James and Joseph, Joanna, wife of Herod's steward, and the sisters Mary and Martha. Others whose names aren't told us show by their acts their devotion to Jesus, such as the woman who anointed his head with expensive ointment, over the protests of his male followers, just before his death (Matt. 26:6-13). We know more about these women than we do about some of the Twelve.

Other unnamed women are prominent because of the compassion that Jesus showed to them. There was the woman healed of a long-standing hemorrhage by touching the fringe of Jesus' garment. There was the Canaanite woman whose persistent faith led Jesus to heal her daughter. Luke tells of a woman who was cured by Jesus of a crippling illness that had left her bent for eighteen years. John tells of the Samaritan woman who gave Jesus a drink of water and received "living water."

These and other women moved through Jesus' life, at times to serve him and at times to be served by him. The full extent of the change that was made by their relationship to Jesus is more often hinted at than spelled out, but one occasion does tell us a great deal.

The story of the sisters Martha and Mary recorded in Luke 10:38-42 has all the ring of the realities of family life. Martha, who had actually invited Jesus into their home, was so deeply involved in the traditional role of the woman as housekeeper that she had no time to attend his teaching; she "was distracted with much serving." By contrast, Mary sat at Jesus' feet and listened to his words. Martha's tension rose until, in a flash of self-righteous anger, she tried to get Jesus to put Mary back to what she considered to be her rightful work: "Lord, do you not care that my sister has left me to serve alone? Tell her then to help me." The complaint is one that strikes a responsive chord in anyone who has been stuck, one time too many, with the dirty dishes in the church kitchen, while others sit, if not at the feet of the speaker, at least around the head table, to get some new truth.

Jesus' instant response to this question is revealing. He advised Martha to leave the dishes and to join Mary at his feet. "But the Lord answered her, 'Martha, Martha, you are anxious and troubled about many things; one thing is needful. Mary has chosen the good portion, which shall not be taken away from her'." Martha was not to be a second-class citizen in the kingdom of God, destined to get her faith from those who belonged next to Jesus while she was to belong in the kitchen. Mary had broken with her traditionally-defined role as keeper of the house. She chose to break with the male domination of access to God. She put herself in a firsthand relationship with Jesus. And Jesus' word is clear and plain, "Mary has chosen the good portion, which shall not be taken from her."

Access to God in ancient Judaism, as well as in most other religions of the time, was dominated by an exclusively male priesthood. These ancient societies were shaped around the ideal of a select group of men who had access to the grace and power of God. Everyone else was subordinate to them. Against all this Jesus launched a kind of silent revolution. He taught, "The kingdom of God is in the midst of you." It was for Martha and Mary no farther away than the person of Jesus as he sat in their home. Old conceptions of a woman's place or her proper role must not be barriers to direct and personal encounter with the freeing presence of Jesus. What does this mean in our day as the risen Christ is in the world calling all to immediate communion with him?

A Hymn of Liberation

A perhaps more significant example of liberation in the Gospels is Mary, the mother of Jesus. Reared by such a mother, it is no wonder, humanly speaking, that he advocated liberation for all people. Yet too often when people have looked to the stories about Mary, they have concluded that she is more part of the problem than part of the answer. Is it not just those virtues of submission and humility that are at the heart of the problem of women's liberation?

To jump to this conclusion is to forget the striking ways in which the early church celebrated Mary as a central actor in the liberation movement God had set loose in the world through Jesus Christ. The New Testament tells the story of Mary in part by means of some great hymns which were probably sung at one time as part of the early Christian worship services. The early church saw Mary as the starting point for the redemption in Christ that was to reach out to the whole world. Her attitude of accepting God's call to be the mother of Jesus was a kind of model for everyone who would respond to the call of God:

> My soul proclaims the greatness of the Lord
> and my spirit exults in God my saviour;
> because he has looked upon his lowly handmaid.
> Yes, from this day forward all generations will call me blessed,
> for the Almighty has done great things for me.
> Holy is his name,
> and his mercy reaches from age to age for those who fear him.
> He has shown the power of his arm,
> he has routed the proud of heart.
> He has pulled down princes from their thrones and exalted the
>   lowly.
> The hungry he has filled with good things, the rich sent empty
>   away.
> He has come to the help of Israel his servant, mindful of his
>   mercy—
> according to the promise he made to our ancestors—
> of his mercy to Abraham and to his descendants for ever.
> (Luke 1:46-55, JB)

Mary's hymn is about liberation. All the wonderfully strong language of the prophets of ancient Israel is found there. God "has shown the power of his arm." The proud are set into disarray. Princes are thrown down; the hungry are fed; the rich are judged; the ancient promises to Abraham are fulfilled. But there is a crucial difference here. There is no mention of attacking armies or terrible battles or legions of avenging angels. The liberation is taking place through a "lowly handmaid." Here is a complete reversal of the ways in which people are accustomed to thinking about God's actions in judgment and redemption. The focus is not on a great king or

prince who liberates the people. The focus is on what God is doing
in and through a young woman. Mary was, at it were, the entering
wedge of God's liberation movement that would culminate in the
fulfillment of God's kingdom. God's eternal purpose for humankind
took on new momentum through Mary at Nazareth.

Mary herself had already gone through the wonderful transformation that is promised to all people by God. She exults in the
new being that comes from God. "My soul proclaims the greatness
of the Lord and my spirit exults in God my saviour." God has
already done "great things for me." Mary is no longer among the
downtrodden but had been called into the ranks of the liberated and
liberating people of God. Listen to the women's liberation language
of the hymn, "Yes, from this day forward all generations will call
me blessed," and of the words of the angel Gabriel, "Hail, O favored
one, the Lord is with you."

There was with Mary a genuine rejoicing in the glory of
God's transforming power. She evidenced none of the false humility
that is in reality nothing but crippling self-hate. Mary had entered
into new power and greatness, and she could rejoice in it. Having
been humble before God, she was liberated from the self-hatred that
is the source of captivity. Having bowed before God, she did not
need to bow before any man. Mary was free of the old life that
allows a person no right to rejoice in the gifts God has given.

Is there not a vital difference between the overbearing egotism
of the insecure and frightened person pointing nervously at his or
her own powers, and the genuine rejoicing of knowing that God can
work wonderful things through you? Reread the great hymn of Mary
in this light. You will be able to see in a new way how Mary shows
that women do not stand at the fringe of God's liberation movement
but at its very center. The hymn calls on all women today to be free
and to rejoice in the real strengths they have.

The Line of Witnesses

Like the other liberation movements whose roots are in the
coming of Jesus Christ, the liberation of women did not at once
win many advocates who shared the vision of Mary of Nazareth,
Joanna, Martha and Mary, and the others. In the early church, as

talked about in Acts, there were the four daughters of Philip the
evangelist who taught the church through their gift of prophecy.
They were church leaders who spoke out of a direct inspiration from
God the word the churches needed to hear (Acts 21:9). Priscilla's
name precedes that of her husband as they instruct the eloquent
Apollos (Acts 18:26). Other women expressed their new freedom
in Christ through lives of service: Dorcas was famed for her sewing
(Acts 9:36ff.); and Timothy's mother, Eunice, and grandmother,
Lois, were exemplars of faith and faithfulness (2 Tim. 1:5). During
the times of persecution, Christian women made their witness in acts
of martyrdom. Yet women were progressively excluded from positions of leadership. The heavy impression of their Jewish or Roman
background made it difficult for early Christians to grasp the radical
newness of things brought about by the life, death, and resurrection
of Jesus.

Then, as now, tradition argued, "But we have never done it that
way in this church before." This contradiction runs throughout
Paul's writings. While he wrote the most radical statement in the
New Testament about how life in Christ dissolves the distinction
of slave and free, Jew and Gentile, male and female (Gal. 3:28),
yet he could also say that women should be silent in church (1 Cor.
14:34-36).

When seeking guidance on these issues, we have to be clear.
Which is more basic: the traditions of the churches or the liberating
work that has its start in Jesus Christ? First century disciples, like
twentieth century disciples, had difficulty in finding the full meaning
of what God has done through the life, death, and resurrection of
Jesus Christ. How clearly do we see the full implications of that
liberation? How do we do justice to Jesus' attitude and acts and to
such passages as Galatians 3:28 as we read and study a Bible that
shows God at work but at work in a male-dominated culture, a
culture which it inevitably reflected?

The history of the church has many stories of brave and
faithful women whose voices have been heard from time to time
in high places. Thus Catherine of Sienna, in the fourteenth century,
was given not only to mystical vision but also to hard-headed politics.

She forced a reluctant pope out of exile and back to Rome. She campaigned long and hard and with convincing passion against papal and courtly corruption.

Others could be added to the list, but too often they were lonely voices. It was one of these lonely voices, Sarah M. Grimke, in nineteenth century America, who had that same vision of God's liberating work that had been given to Mary of Nazareth. The daughter of a slave-holding family in South Carolina, Sarah rebelled and joined the Society of Friends because of their leadership in opposing slavery. By 1836 she and her sister Angelina founded the American Anti-Slavery Society.

But as Sarah Grimke struggled for the liberation of the slaves, she found herself caught in another liberation struggle. It was for the liberation of women, so they could take their place of leadership against the evils of their day. Many people were willing to let women entertain ideas about the liberation of slaves in private, but they were certainly not to express them in public. Sarah's public speaking in the churches called forth a letter of censure from the ministers' association. Her answer to this letter from the General Association of Congregational Ministers is a classic. In it she tells how all of God's works of liberation are finally linked together.

> I rejoice, because I am persuaded that the rights of woman, like the rights of slaves, need only be examined to be understood and asserted. . . .
> The motto of woman when she is engaged in the great work of public reformation should be, "The Lord is my light and my salvation. Whom shall I fear? The Lord is the strength of my life. Of whom shall I be afraid?"
> She must feel, if she feels rightly, that she is fulfilling one of the important duties laid upon her as an accountable being, and that her character, instead of being "unnatural," is in exact accordance with the will of God to whom, and to no other, she is responsible for the talents and the gifts confided to her.[6]

As a modern teacher of the church, Catherine Gonzalez, put it, "It is not only for the sake of women that their subjection must be ended. . . . It is instead for the sake of the church—that the redemption it proclaims may be lived, that the gospel may be believed by the whole world." [7]

There is a wholeness to Christ's work of liberation. All are finally to be one in him. How is Christ's work of liberation breaking out in new ways in your midst?

8

King of Righteousness or Rule Giver?

One of our most common complaints today is about the decline and fall of morals in our world. The scandals of political intrigue and bribery have just about numbed us with their severity and frequency. Theft and violence have confined our lives behind locked doors, barbed wire fences, guards, and guns. Sexual morality has tumbled into a confusion where the virtues of marital fidelity or chastity are pushed aside as quaint reminders of a vanished past. We fear worse may lie ahead, for our human moral laws have a way of slowly dissolving and disappearing from sight when they are repeatedly broken.

Amid this confusion, men and women are looking afresh for land-marks that show a path to order and life and away from chaos and death. In this search, whether carried out by young or old, in the East or the West, among Christians or non-Christians, Jesus is repeatedly hailed as one whose word may be the saving word for which people are seeking. Even those who launch strong criticisms of the traditional Christian claims for Jesus as Savior and Lord often point to his ethical teachings as a source of hope. Above all the arguments over doctrines of the incarnation or atonement, one assertion seems to stand unchallenged: Jesus was a great ethical teacher.

Certainly this is apparent in the New Testament. Major collections of Jesus' ethical teaching are found there, the largest and most familiar of which is of course the so-called Sermon on the Mount (Matt. 5—7). Yet Jesus' words have touched people in a host of conflicting ways.

In response to the demands of Jesus' ethic, some, like young

conflict.

Luther, have gone off to the monastery, seeking to be free of temptation and distraction so they can more fully live up to his standard. Others have felt called by these same words to service in distant lands. Thus Albert Schweitzer said, "I have come to Africa in response to a commandment of Christ."

Mahatma Gandhi, the great Hindu leader, found in the Sermon on the Mount the roots of his doctrine of non-violence. In like spirit Tom Rodd, a young anti-war demonstrator, refused compliance with the draft law during the Vietnam War because of his allegiance to the ethics of Jesus. He willingly went to jail in order to keep clear of compromise with Jesus' ethic of peace. In contrast Dietrich Bonhoeffer was moved to join the anti-Nazi freedom fighters in Germany during World War II in response to the ethical imperatives of Jesus.

Most of us, however, caught up in the ordinances of everyday life, far from heroism and martyrdom, are left to wonder. What does it mean to live under the ethic of a teacher who said, "Enter by the narrow gate. The gate is wide that leads to perdition, there is plenty of room on the road, and many go that way; but the gate that leads to life is small and the road is narrow, and those who find it are few"? (Matt. 7:13-14, NEB) We have seen that it is hard to follow Jesus the Liberator; is the moral teacher any easier to obey? What does he really expect of us who are his disciples?

Being Honest About Ourselves

A good place to start is by looking carefully at how Jesus defined his own role in regard to human morality. Where does he start when he calls for ethical faithfulness? This method is far more profitable than blaming others for our moral crisis.

It is easy to blame others. One of the favorite words used by some, especially the young, to describe the moral breakdown in the world is "hypocrisy." With unbending zeal, they apply their ethical ideals unsparingly to the world they know, laying bare its contradictions. A nation espouses peace, they say, but carries on war. A church preaches brotherhood but practices segregation. The list could be extended greatly, but it is already well known.

Others, usually older, speak from their places of responsibility in the status-quo world of everyday life and speak differently. They refer to a "disregard for moral values." They point out that the young who upbraid them for hypocrisy accept adultery, homosexuality, and revolutionary violence as part of people's right "to do their own thing." It is clear, the voices of the establishment argue, that no new order can be built on a disregard for moral values, no matter how riddled with hypocrisy the old order may seem to be.

Both parties to this argument lay claim to Jesus and his ethic as the source of their moral critique and the basis of their hope for the future. We are alternately urged onward to that "brave new tomorrow" in which the teachings of Jesus will be followed by all, or we are told to go back to the "good old days" when people believed in the ethic of Jesus.

The impasse in this debate does not come because one side is right and the other wrong. It comes because both parties to the debate miss the point that Jesus himself sought to make. The true meaning of Jesus' ethics can never be found by joining moral criticism of others to the assurance of one's own goodness. The mystery of Jesus' ethic is unlocked from the perspective of the self-criticism that Jesus called repentance. The starting point for Jesus' ethic is people being more sensitive to their own "hypocrisy" and to their own "disregard for moral values" than to others'.

Before he ever undertook any moral instruction, Jesus first came preaching, "Repent, and believe the gospel." He first invited people into discipleship with him through repentance and faith, and then he talked about the ethical directions this new style of life demanded. Ethics are to grow out of a new life relationship, not just from new moral ideas. It was not ethics first, followed by faith. Nor did he teach, as we sometimes seem to do, that if you believe a great deal you can be permitted a certain indifference to social ethics. Yet he did not have any part in the notion that vigorous social action excuses people from a deep and serious faith. Rather Jesus held the two together. Love of God and love of neighbor are finally all of a piece.

Jesus understood the psychology of morality far better than most of us ever do. He summed it up in a simple saying: "For no good tree bears bad fruit, nor again does a bad tree bear good fruit; for each tree is known by its own fruit. For figs are not gathered from thorns, nor are grapes picked from a bramble bush. The good man out of the good treasure of his heart produces good, and the evil man out of his evil treasure produces evil; for out of the abudance of the heart his mouth speaks." (Luke 6:43-45) Having entered into a new relationship with him through faith, the old self starts to die, the new self in Christ begins to come to life, and the new moral life begins. Our usual efforts at moral reform, from a New Year's resolution to the decision to avoid extra calories, tend to be only temporary and cosmetic in their results. It is like binding figs on a thorn tree, or grapes on a bramble bush. They may look great for the moment, but they won't last and they can never repeat themselves.

Games People Play

This approach to ethics as the fruit of faith was as unwelcome to many in Jesus' day as it is to many now. Unlike our own time, there was then no crisis of moral values among the Jews. Certainly people did not always do the right, but there were commonly acknowledged standards of right and wrong. It was a matter of divine revelation. God had revealed his law. Now learned interpreters worked to define and redefine its exact implications for their everyday life.

At the heart of the Jewish ethical system stood the Ten Commandments and the many laws of the Torah—the first five books of the Bible. A complex legal system had been built up slowly on the basis of these revealed laws of God by interpretations that sought to fit them to the ever new circumstances under which people were living. Rabbis of great learning and sanctity sought to help people avoid the uncertainty of not knowing what to do by ever extending the rule of law to every nook and cranny of life.

Jesus came into this world, so free of moral uncertainty, and created a moral crisis. The critics of Jesus were very clear on this point. He had thrown their finely tuned ethical system completely into disarray. Jesus' critics said that he had "poured scorn on the words of the wise men, led the people astray, and claimed that he had not come to take something away from the Law, but to add something to it." [8] What did he do?

When Jesus first started teaching, the people sensed they were hearing something radically new. "And they were astonished at his teaching, for he taught them as one who had authority, and not as the scribes." "What is this? A new teaching!" (Mark 1:22 and 27) Unlike the scribes, who thought like well-trained lawyers, Jesus did not weigh one opinion against another and then arrive at an opinion. Instead, he spoke with a sudden and direct personal authority. He spoke not as a new legal interpreter, but as a king.

Jesus always stressed his complete dependence on the law *Jesus &* of God. He did not want to do away with the law. He told the *the law* people, "Till heaven and earth disappear, not one dot, not one little stroke, shall disappear from the Law until its purpose is achieved." (Matt. 5:18, JB) Jesus' aim rather was to unlock its inner meaning and power. Many people around him were unable either to accept or understand just what he meant. All they could sense was the newness and power of his teaching, and they feared he was destroying the great ethical system handed down by their fathers.

In the effort to render the meaning of the law exactly clear for every situation, the traditional interpreters had surrounded it with a complex set of "do's and don'ts." These were sometimes called "the hedge around the law." The idea was that if you would follow these secondary rules and regulations you would be spared the danger of ever violating God's commandments themselves. The problem was that this "hedge around the law" had turned into underbrush obscuring the law. Jesus undertook a prophetic criticism of these human traditions, the word of man, in order to make plain the Word of God.

All of us are apt to take the law and turn it into a kind of fetish. The law on tithing was a favorite. Tithing had been refined to the nth degree in Jesus' day. Religious people had even taken to tithing the table spices when they sat down to dinner—they put aside a tenth part of the mint and dill and cummin as holy unto the Lord. Jesus did not simply condone this as a kind of silly piety. He took it with great seriousness. It was serious because preoccupation with these legal niceties had obscured far bigger and more important issues. Hence this kind of piety was downright dangerous in Jesus' view. "Woe to you, scribes and Pharisees, hypocrites! for you tithe

mint and dill and cummin, and have neglected the weightier matters
of the law, justice and mercy and faith; these you ought to have done,
without neglecting the others." (Matt. 23:23) In a strange way,
what people had counted as their morality had become a block to
seeing what God was actually demanding of them.

Jesus condemned this kind of morality as hypocrisy. The word
"hypocrite" is an important one in Jesus' ethical teaching. The
Greek word from which we get "hypocrite" meant "actor," one
who, on stage, pretended to be what he was not. Religious hypocrites
were the people who tried to appear righteous because they had
observed the rules for hand washing, tithing, diet, worshiping, and
sabbath observance, while all the time they lived a life of prideful
scorn and self-centeredness. Morality was a kind of playacting that
obscured their real selves.

Hypocrisy is one of the most dangerous games people play, and
it is not one limited just to Jesus' day. By taking on the solemn mask
and dark garb of religiousness, it becomes possible to elude God's
real claim on us. Our moral guilt springs from the prejudice, fear,
apathy, and arrogance that lurk behind the facade of conventional
respectability.

A modern psychiatrist, Eric Berne, described human behavior
in terms of *Games People Play*.[9] People try to control those around
them by acting out a role to which others will respond. What Jesus
was doing was to expose the "morality game" in which most of us
are involved, for it is one to which religious people are particularly
addicted. In it, we all become actors, "hypocrites," to use Jesus'
word. We try to gain status before God and our neighbors by
following all the rules of the religous life and conventional morality.
Yet, at the same time, we resist the inner transformation of love and
trust to which Jesus calls his disciples.

The morality game can take some extreme and demanding
forms. Jesus warned about the zeal of those who "traverse sea and
land to make a single proselyte, and when he becomes a proselyte,
you make him twice as much a child of hell as yourselves." (Matt.
23:15) Paul warns about that extreme form of "the morality game"
in which "I give away all I have," and "deliver my body to be

burned," while still living in pride and hatred (1 Cor. 13:3). But if we lack love, he says, this counts for nothing.

Strangely enough, ethics interpreted as living up to the rules has often tended to fuel the self-righteous pride that is the denial of the justice and love of God. Jesus is saying that no matter how well we play "the morality game," we are really unmasked actors. We have no real self left before God or other people. The only ones that accept you for your skill in the "morality game" are those who are trying to play it along with you. It is simply not possible to substitute regular church-going and tithing for love of neighbor and forgiveness of enemies. Jesus brought to an end the kind of moral calculation that balances off our moral strong points against our weak ones. Jesus is the enemy of all forms of legalism, including those thought up by Christians.

Inside or Outside

Jesus, then, is the great teacher of ethics. Before, however, we are ready to walk the path of obedience, we must admit our unworthiness and commit ourselves to Jesus and his forgiving grace. Otherwise by our acts we profess a godliness that we do not possess, and we are hypocrites.

But Jesus struck more deeply into the problem of human morality than this. He forced people to look from their actions to the motives behind the actions. "You have heard that it was said to the men of old, 'You shall not kill. . . .' But I say to you that everyone who is angry with his brother shall be liable to judgment; . . . and whoever says, 'You fool!' shall be liable to the hell of fire." (Matt. 5:21-22) In saying this, Jesus was forcing us to face the problem: does morality come from inside or outside of us?

Much of our language about morals betrays a strange misunderstanding. We speak of "cracking down on law and order" or "tightening up on morals." We seem to think that morality is something that can be forced on someone from the outside. We act as if some promise or threat makes people good. But it is clear that threat can produce only outward conformity. This is valuable for society, since laws on moral issues help prevent violence, discrimination, etc. But neither promise nor threats can produce moral goodness before God.

If we look at Jesus' ethical teachings in this new light, perhaps we can make sense out of some of the seemingly confusing things we find in the Gospels. Jesus repeatedly takes the usual laws of morality and reinterprets them in such a way that they seem to have become impossible to obey, for he makes them incredibly severe. Most of us feel we can handle our temptations to commit murder and adultery. We may have some doubts about our ability to resist the temptations to retaliation and swearing, but given stern effort we tend to believe we can handle these as well. On our better days, we think we can even show love of neighbor. But Jesus says clearly that this kind of morality simply will not do.

> You have heard that is was said to the men of old, "You shall not kill; and whoever kills shall be liable to judgment." But I say to you that every one who is angry with his brother shall be liable to judgment; whoever insults his brother shall be liable to the council, and whoever says, "You fool!" shall be liable to the hell of fire. (Matt. 5:21-22)
> You have heard that it was said, "You shall not commit adultery." But I say to you that every one who looks at a woman lustfully has already committed adultery with her in his heart. (Matt. 5:27-28)

The list could be lengthened, as Jesus made radical the demands of God on us. Love must extend not only to neighbor but to enemy as well. Retaliation is not just to be forgotten; it must be replaced by a willingness to serve those who put unreasonable demands upon us. What are we to make of all this?

Trying to police our inner thoughts so as to free ourselves of anger or lust is clearly a slow if not impossible business. Jesus is not urging his disciples to a kind of emotional repression. What he really wants is something very different. Jesus wants us to face and admit the old self in each one of us. True, we can sometimes tidy up our outward actions. (And thank God we do!) But Jesus wanted to keep us in touch with reality. Beneath our outwardly respectable exteriors, attitudes such as fear, hatred, lust, and greed, which are the source of evil deeds, are still present. What Jesus was trying to make us see is that we cannot handle these forces on our own. In repentance and faith, this old self has to die and the new self take its place. But this rebirth is not within our powers. It comes when we relate to Jesus himself. (Compare what was said about this on p. 49 ff.)

cf. Ethics impossible as a do-it yourself effort.

In his ethical teaching, Jesus is cutting us off from the last possibility of self-righteousness by showing the need for that deeper victory over the self that only he can bring. This is why Jesus warns us, "I tell you, unless you show yourselves far better men than the Pharisees and the doctors of the law, you can never enter the kingdom of Heaven." (Matt. 5:20, NEB) Morality starts from the inside and works outward, not the other way around. Here is where the basic change is taking place. "Wicked thoughts, murder, adultery, fornication, theft, perjury, slander—these all proceed from the heart; and these are the things that defile a man. . . ." (Matt. 15:19-20, NEB)

The key to morality is not yet another attempt to force a lagging will, but an attempt to find a new center for life. This is why Jesus always addressed his ethical teachings to his disciples primarily, not to the merely curious crowds. It is not the attempt to follow Jesus' ethics that makes people disciples and introduces them to the kingdom of God; it starts the other way round. When a person lives by faith, he or she is starting to share in the kingdom of God already. Then he is ready to hear the pattern of life of those who have accepted the reign of God as the basis for living. Jesus' ethic is not the prescription for working your way into heaven. It is the expression of the heaven he has put in you when you become his disciple. Jesus' ethic is the ethic of grace.

In the famous parable of the last judgment, Jesus lays bare the real sources of human morality. God the King sits on his throne of judgment with humankind arrayed before him. He separates the righteous from the unrighteous. When the righteous are called into the eternal blessings of the kingdom, they are genuinely surprised. They say, "Lord, when did we see thee hungry and feed thee, or thirsty and give thee drink?" (Matt. 25:37) They were capable of genuine love because they had not first set out to gain status before God. They were not consciously seeking their own salvation. They were simply responding in love to the human needs they saw around them. "And the King will answer them, 'Truly, I say to you, as you did it to one of the least of these my brethren, you did it to me.' " (Matt. 25:40)

By contrast, the unrighteous are afflicted with a strange blindness. Like the righteous they will reply, "Lord, when was it that we saw you hungry or thirsty or a stranger or naked or ill or in prison, and did nothing for you?" (Matt. 25:44, NEB) Having encountered in the world no one that they recognized as being the Lord, the unrighteous were willing to ignore the crying need of those around them and went about their business as usual. So the parable concludes with a word of doom. " 'I tell you this: anything you did not do for one of these, however humble, you did not do for me.' And they will go to eternal punishment, but the righteous will enter eternal life." (Matt. 25:46, NEB)

The basis of morality is the transforming grace that allows us to perceive the acts of love to be done right now. The inability to perceive the deed of love that is required is itself sin. That radical self-centeredness that blinds us to God's call in a world of needy people has, according to Jesus, fatal results—"they will go away to eternal punishment."

When Jesus taught in Palestine, and now as he teaches us as risen Lord, his message is first and foremost the call to repentance and faith. Then as people respond to him in faith, they are ready to ethical instruction.

Often we are impatient with this ordering of things. We say, "I want a simple religion. I don't want all this talk of grace and forgiveness. I just want to try to live by the Sermon on the Mount." If you read the Sermon on the Mount with care, it would soon be clear that such a religion would be anything but simple.

But Jesus has moved ethics away from being a list of "do's and don'ts" to a call for a whole new self. So it would be misleading to bring together some set of rules that are Jesus' rules. What we need to do instead is to look at the forms of new life he is giving us in our time. We need to find those places where the pressures and problems of our time are driving people to dead-end streets of immorality, fear, hatred, and violence, and then see how Christ is leading us to the new possibilities of ministry. To go back to Jesus' parable, we need to find the hungry, thirsty, lonely, naked, ill, and imprisoned of this world because they are God's signposts to where the new life in Christ must be brought. We need to find these people and the problems that have brought them low, because this is where the new life in Christ must take its shape. Where do you see these people today?

9 | Jesus and Spaceship Earth

One of the newest areas of ethical questioning for the disciples of Jesus in the twentieth century is that of ecology. Ecology, though a relatively new word to most of us, already has led to frenzied concern and heated arguments. Shortages of fuel and scarcities of goods are no longer terrors projected for the future, but facts of everyday life. Poisoned air and water are no longer distant and impersonal facts for biologists or sociologists, but matters of "life and breath" for us all.

"Ecology" comes from the Greek word that means "house." Ecology is the science of this vast house in which we live—the world and everyone in it. And a house, no matter how large, is not limitless in its resources or in the room it provides for waste and spoilage. Eventually, everyone in the house has to take seriously the existence of everyone else. We simply can't go on living in the house as if we were the only people there.

Hence we are in an "ecological crisis," or, to put it simply, we are in a crisis over the house in which we live—the earth. Waste disposal, clean air, and the exploiting of natural resources are issues that affect us and our future. Since people are so vitally touched, Jesus' disciples must ask, where is Christ to be encountered and served in relationship to such problems?

We are crowding ever closer to one another as the population explosion threatens to squeeze us off the earth. The intensity of life in the great urban centers increases year by year as human lives are piled on top of one another in high rise apartments and as people elbow one another in crowded streets. Even for those who live in the country, pollution moves in ominously from the urban centers on air currents, in rivers, and in garbage trucks or even garbage trains.

One by one the frontiers of the world have disappeared. The "vast empty spaces" are filling up. The spaciousness of our world has disappeared. While the United States still offers us some vast vistas of open countryside, it is possible to cross large parts of the earth and never be outside the sight or sound of human life. Scientists now speak of the world as a tightly packed spaceship hurtling through space and time, a spaceship that must keep its ecological balance and handle carefully its resources or become a lifeless shell.

Despite all this physical concentration of human beings, there remains a paradox. Our world is the world of the lonely. The urban masses are not pressed into deeper relationships with one another. They are, instead, the lonely crowd. Sheer physical closeness does not bring community; rather, it often deepens tensions and rubs raw nerves to open aggression. Some people, unable to bear the press of other lives about them, withdraw into a private world of illusion and emotional retreat. The question is, how do we find new ways to live together? The search for community has stopped being a pleasant dream for our spare time and has become an urgent necessity.

Within our homes and churches, the search for community has a kind of pathetic intensity. Families, their sensitivities dulled by long familiarity, mask their fear of really knowing one another by overly busy schedules of going hither and yon. Churches mask their lack of oneness behind stiffly formal worship services, followed by the shallow togetherness of the coffee hour, usually spent in a room called a fellowship hall that too often offers no fellowship at all. Even our piety often tends to stress the exclusiveness of our individual communion with God. All of this seems a tragic forgetting of what life in Christ is meant to be.

The earliest disciples of Jesus found out something new about their relationships to one another. They were not simply a group of individuals who happened to believe in Jesus; they were members of his body. They learned that their relationships to one another were not an optional extra with which they could dispense if they liked.

And they believed the kind of relationship they had with one another in Christ was what God intended the whole world to share and enjoy.

"The Whole World in His Hand"

To be in Christ is to share in his body. It is to be under his headship. It is to be joined to others by being joined with Christ. The New Testament pictures all of this in the widest terms. What was happening among the disciples was going to reach out to embrace the whole world. The risen Christ would build a new humanity in himself. He would reach to us who were "strangers and sojourners" and knit us into a new community that would break through the barriers of space and race and clan to form "a holy temple in the Lord" (Eph. 2:19-22). We can confidently expect this because in Jesus Christ "all things hold together," and because God was pleased "through him to reconcile to himself all things" (Col. 1:17, 20). A simple Christian faith captures this mystery in the song that celebrates the good news that "he's got the whole world in his hands."

There are two contrasting convictions in all Christian belief about Jesus Christ. On the one hand, the Christian is concerned with the person of Jesus Christ. He is known personally and spoken of in the intimate terms of human relationship. On the other hand, Christian faith speaks of this same Jesus Christ in great, overarching terms. He is the eternal Word of God, the first-born of all creation and the sustainer of the universe (John 1:1; Col. 1:15; Heb. 1:3). He is God's agent of creation and will be the consummation of the universe. No matter how far human imagination goes in picturing the outer reaches of space, no matter how far into the future imagination stretches toward a world of moon stations and space travel, we will never outrun the presence of Jesus Christ.

In science there is a mystery as to what holds all things together. The key to this mystery for the Christian is to be found finally in the power of love revealed in the dying and rising of Christ. Ancient Christians expressed this beautifully in the mosaic pictures they put in their churches. One of the greatest of these mosaics shows Christ the King, enthroned against a background of gold, reigning high above the earth and the heavens. But the hands he holds out in kingly power over the universe are the nail-pierced hands of the crucified.

What the mosaic tells us is that the hope of the world, in the face of all that destroys life, is revealed in Jesus Christ. The man we know personally, the one who died in first century Palestine, is the key to everything human beings can ever know or hope for. Wherever humankind goes, we will encounter the crucified and risen one. When we search for the way to live together in the future, we must look to him, for he is the head of the new humanity that is coming into existence. The staggering problems that cloud the way to the future have not run beyond the resources of Jesus Christ, because "in him all things hold together." To have new life in Christ is to insure not being left behind by a world moving toward the future, for it is sharing in him who is shaping the future.

To measure our search for new and deeper forms of human community against this understanding of Christ is to find the light that is needed. Jesus is not simply the great and good teacher of the past from whom we are moving so rapidly. He is the Lord already in the future ready to meet us there. Sometimes timid disciples have been defensive about the future and doggedly determined not to change anything. This is a denial of the power of Christ. We dare not minimize the problems that confront us on spaceship earth now. We must face the fact that every indication is that overcrowding and under-resourcing will get worse. But we also must face our fears and hopes for the future as disciples of the Lord of the future. Let's look in detail at the two related points of concern that have already been mentioned: the potentially destructive effect of over-crowding and the human hunger for community.

Beehives or Families

The sheer pressure of people on one another today makes the notion of rugged individualism a thing of the past. No one can live to himself and disregard others. There is simply not enough room or resources left for this kind of life. We have to take seriously the responsibilities we have for one another, or the tragic consequences of our disregard will overwhelm us.

Yet whenever we start to think in these terms, a fear overtakes us. Are we to be regimented into some kind of degrading collective society? What happens to people when they are forced to live in mass dictatorial societies is all too evident. In the twentieth century, the attempts of fascism and communism to create new societies have shown how quickly persons can become dehumanized. Against all of this we cry out, "For goodness' sake, leave me alone!" We all shun a future in which we are forced to live like bees in a hive. To be forced into one mold, allowed to think only one thought, and given but one niche in which to live would not be life. It would be a kind of subhuman existence. We rightly fear such a future.

The pattern for life together given in Jesus Christ is of a very different sort. Its starting point, however, is the same. Men and women are not made to live alone. As human beings we belong together. In Christ we are brought together in a new way. However, we have tended to get badly confused on this point. We like to start thinking about ourselves and our own needs and our own individual relationship to God, and then we plan to think about how we might relate to others. Is not the problem of thinking this way that we seldom get beyond our own rights and needs to those of others?

The new life in Christ points in a different direction. We must live a new kind of life together because of the way we belong to Christ. Our relationship to him inevitably puts us in a new kind of community, called both the body of Christ and the household or family of God. Christian faith believes in a collective life for disciples, but it is not the collective of the beehive or rabbit hutch, which obliterates individuality. It is the collective or community of the body and of the family.

One of the basic problems that has confronted the church since its beginnings is to know how to live together in Christ. Many disciples clearly have wanted to make of their new community in Christ just a continuation of their way of living before Christ. For example, James and John, with the help of their mother, tried to stake out positions of leadership for themselves (Mark 10:35-45). They were rejecting community life in the body of Christ for the old pyramid of power. Nor are they alone in wanting to be at the top of the heap; the church often has been troubled with bitter fights over just who would be first. But to bring the worldly principle of domination into the life of the church is inconsistent with the spirit of the new community that is being formed in Christ.

The community in Christ recognizes real and important differences between people. But it does not make these differences the basis for a judgment of higher or lower, better or worse. Rather, the new community is described in terms of a body whose parts are all different but all indispensible to each other. Paul carries through this point with eloquence to the Corinthians when he tells them, "If the foot should say, 'Because I am not a hand, I do not belong to the body,' that would not make it less a part of the body. . . . If the whole body were an eye, where would be the hearing? If the whole body were an ear, where would be the sense of smell?" (1 Cor. 12:15, 17)

Each member of the body has its own dignity and importance. It becomes part of the whole not by being denied its uniqueness, but by placing its unique contribution into the services of the whole. A body exists through the special contribution of each of its parts. Each part has its meaning and purpose in supplying the needs of the body as a whole.

The new community in which we share by faith is the body of Christ. In it all people have their dignity and importance. All bring to it those gifts that are uniquely their own. People are not forced to be identical to one another in Christ. Each one is to find the ways in which his or her own particular self fits into the whole. The thing that *is* blocked by being in Christ is using your own gifts for self-centered purposes. The headship in this body belongs to Christ.

Already in the world around us we can start to see what life together in a body can mean for the future of humankind. In our commuties today various minority groups are finding value and beauty in their differences from the prevailing patterns. Youth, blacks, and the so-called "ethnic minorities" (Polish, Italian, Japanese, etc.) have discovered that their life-style or heritage is not a kind of mistake to be overcome but a value to be cherished. More and more people are beginning to learn that these differences are not threatening or annoying. Everyone doesn't have to be exactly alike. All the people in our neighborhood don't have to have identical life patterns.

Christians can start to realize how much the Biblical picture of our life together in a body has to say to us. Does it not mean accepting the differences among us and finding the special contribution others have to make, instead of trying to make them over into carbon copies of ourselves?

The Household of God

By being related to Christ people are brought into a new household or family. ". . . You are no longer strangers and so-journers, but you are fellow citizens with the saints and members of the household of God. . . ." (Eph. 2:19) Those who are in Christ are part of an extended family that reaches over the barriers of time and space. In a family all members are fulfilled and find true life by sharing in the life of the family as a whole, while still being themselves. The father is not the son, nor is the sister the brother. The model of Christian community is not that of a machine with identical and replaceable cogs. It is a family that respects the special way in which God has created each one of us.

Yet too often this model of the family breaks down; family life is destroyed by hostility. Whether it be the family in your own house, or the family of God in your local church, or the larger family of God throughout the world, hostility is a grim reality.

The New Testament speaks of a "dividing wall of hostility." (Eph. 2:14) In the New Testament church "the dividing wall of hostility" was between Jews and Gentiles. It is a tragic wall that is with us still. Anti-semitism still draws strength from the perverted faith of Christians who forget Jesus' word, "For salvation is from the Jews." (John 4:22) Faith in Jesus Christ leaves no more room for the polite anti-semitism of American life than for the virulent anti-semitism that kindled the holocaust of Nazism. Our socially acceptable anti-semitism is but the malignant offspring of the horrible anti-semitism we all despise. And petty flames can quickly become consuming fires.

In the churches there is a "dividing wall of hostility" between the liberals and the conservatives. Each time it seems these unseemly fights within the churches are over and done with, they break out afresh. As God's pattern of the body or the family is forgotten, zeal for Christ gets mistranslated into an implacable opposition to other Christians.

In the home, there is sometimes a wall between parents and children. It may be just the annoying barrier between a father and son who simply cannot hear one another for shouting past each other. Or it may be the hostility of the waspish words between a mother and daughter who cannot resist carping criticism of one another. Tragically, for some it has gone beyond mere harrassment, as with the father who wrote, "My Son, the Enemy." In a true, first-hand report, the father told of a son so lost in the world of drugs and isolated from his family that he finally attacked his parents and was killed by his father in self-defense.

What has been said about the church and the family could be applied with equal truth to the world community, where there is a wall between East and West, rich and poor, developed and developing. But it is not as easy to apply the principles of the Christian faith to nations as to families or churches. Yet in Christ the wall has been broken down. Disciples, instead of glaring at one another, should find unity through their common vision of Jesus Christ. Hatred has been overcome because in his death Christ took the hatred into himself and destroyed it. Christ has taken the two parties to our enmities, no matter who they are, and brought them into a new oneness. ". . . In his own body of flesh and blood [he] has broken down the enmity which stood like a dividing wall between them . . . so as to create out of the two a single new humanity in himself, thereby making peace." (Eph. 2:14-16, NEB) The future of humankind lies in entering more fully into the new humanity in Christ. He is the power of unity.

The Dance of Life

Donald Baillie, a great modern teacher of the faith in Scotland, drew a word picture of the new humanity being formed by Christ. He likened humankind to people standing in a great circle facing away from the center. Jesus Christ is the center of the circle, although the people are unaware of this, for their backs are turned on him. Also, because they are turned from the center, they are really not able to see one another, save in distorting glimpses of those on either side of them.

Thus caught up in their own self-centered existence, people do not know the real center and source of life, nor do they really know one another. Each one is bent inward upon himself. The great circle of humanity should be caught up in joyous dance before their Lord, but it is sullen and silent. The most we can seem to manage is a solitary frug or isolated temper tantrum. As Jesus said, "To what then shall I compare the men of this generation, and what are they like? They are like children sitting in the market place and calling to one another, 'We piped to you, and you did not dance. . . .' " (Luke 7:31-32)

But when in repentance and faith people are able to do an about-face, they catch the vision of the living Lord at the center of life. People are drawn to him. As they come ever closer to the center, they come nearer to one another. And now with eyes opened toward Christ, they can truly see one another. The distorting side glimpses that had made their neighbors into strange and threatening foes are replaced by true sight.

Then slowly, tentatively, people reach out their hands to one another. At first, they touch hands in love, and then they link arms together in the dance of life. Having been reconciled to him, men and women are reconciled to one another. It is a time of joy, like a marriage feast. In fact, this is what the New Testament calls it. It is the marriage feast of Jesus, the Lamb of God, with the church, his bride (Rev. 19:7-9).

This is a word picture of what God is doing through Jesus Christ. Like all pictures, we may enjoy its beauty but still doubt its reality. In the places where we live, in our particular church or community or home, the walls of hostility still seem very real. Our hope is grounded in the fact that Jesus Christ is more real still.

This is why Christians have always spoken of him in such wonderful, overarching terms. No puny words are sufficient to the scope of his power or his love. He is called the second person of the Trinity, the creator and sustainer of all that is, the eternal Word of God, the head of the new humanity—his body. He is the Lord of the past, present, and future. These are not mere theological abstractions. They are the ways in which Christians shout for joy. In saying all of these things about Jesus Christ, we are affirming that his reality and power are greater than any power now loose in the world.

No matter how stubborn and resistant this world is to his will, he is stronger yet. No matter how fragmentary and imperfect it seems right now, the community he is building in our midst has a future. It has the only kind of future in which we can hope. It is a community that will grow through him. Its final outcome is certain, no matter what may be its ups and downs in our own times. This surety comes from his power and love. The basic questions remain: Are we willing to be truly responsible inhabitants of spaceship earth? Will we go beyond that to live in love as members of the body of Christ and of the family of faith?

[handwritten notes:]

questions - What does Jesus have to do with us ecology population pollution, scarcity, loliness,

1. Can't escape Christ no matter what the problem. He is all in all.

2. Individualism no longer possible This is frightening We don't want to be messed up in a mass society New humanity in Christ where all individuals count.

3.

10 | The Lord of the Future

A basic question before every human being is, "What does the future hold?" In times of deep human uncertainty like our own, men and women have looked into the future with a mixture of hope and fear. They have tried to pry it open with everything from a fortune teller's crystal ball to electronic computers. Nor is fascination with the clairvoyant who can tell us of the future limited to primitive societies; the popularity in our time of astrology and of Jeanne Dixon makes this clear.

For those who shun such things as superstition and magic, interest in the future is not necessarily dead. A group of top scientists and economists at the Massachusetts Institute of Technology built an elaborate collection of data that was analyzed by intricately programmed computers to forecast the future. What would be our standard of living in the next century? What would the pollution crisis or the population explosion mean for the world of tomorrow? In like fashion the United States government and major corporations spend millions of dollars to find out what life will be like in the year 2000.

Such concern is not merely idle curiosity. Our expectations for the future are a basic factor in how we act today. We must look long and hard at the consequences of what we are doing now, or we may have no future.

Furthermore, each of us is personally concerned with the future because as human beings we all live by hope. Where there is no hope, there is no real life. As Paul says, the source of steadfast and faithful service for Christians is the assurance that our labor is not in vain (1 Cor. 15:58).

The religion of the Hebrews reckoned with the future and its importance for humankind. When the prophets of ancient Israel confronted the people with a word from God, their message spoke of the future. But their words were not intended to satisfy idle curiosity. Amos, Isaiah, and the rest demanded an immediate response from the people because of the judgment God would otherwise bring upon them. The prophet of the Babylonian exile struck a more positive note as he called the people to fresh faith and courage because salvation was soon to come (as in Isa. 40:9-11).

If we turn to the New Testament, it is clear that the future was very important to Jesus and his earliest followers. In fact, it was impossible to talk about religion in first century Palestine without talking about the future. The Zealots hoped for a future to be established by military revolution. The Essenes and many Pharisees dreamed of a future in which God would miraculously intervene to rescue his saints and destroy sinners.

We are often tempted to joke about people who carry signs saying, "It is later than you think," or "The end of the world is near." To many people in Jesus' time, this sort of sentiment was no joking matter. They believed that something decisive was going to happen, and it was going to happen soon. They believed that, the way things were going, the world could not be sustained much longer. God was going to act to do away with the injustice and the oppression and the death they saw at every hand. When Jesus spoke of the time being fulfilled and the kingdom of God at hand, his words struck a deeply responsive chord among them. They were eager to listen.

The whole of the New Testament is filled with teachings about Jesus and the future, from the Gospels through the Letters to the great visions of the future in the Book of Revelation. Even as they prayed, the early Christians looked to the future. They prayed, "thy kingdom come, thy will be done on earth as it is in heaven." They ended their prayers with the fervent shout, *Marana tha,* "Come, Lord." They looked to a future in which Jesus Christ would return to complete his mission of bringing the kingdom of God fully to their midst.

For long periods of time, much of the church has been content to let this whole side of Jesus' message slide from its attention. Such an attitude seems almost inevitable as long as we believe that the world, like "old man river," will just keep "rolling along."

But what happens when the old ways of the world and even of the church are uprooted? What happens when the world is shaken with the fear of imminent nuclear holocaust, ecological crisis, and worldwide famine? To regain an authentic hope that will allow us to live in the present, our eyes turn to the future and to what God will do in it. Despite the fanaticism and misunderstanding that has dogged such efforts, we still must ask, as we did in the last chapter, What does it mean to say that Jesus is Lord of the future?

Wars and Rumors of Wars

Jesus' teachings about the future are a mixture of short-range pessimism and long-range optimism. He does not speak of an easy ascent to the kingdom of God. He speaks instead of "wars and rumors of wars," of "famines and pestilences," of the persecution and betrayal of the faithful (Matt. 24:4-36; Mark 13:5-37; Luke 21:8-36). These tragic events make up the story of humankind.

"Such things are bound to happen; but the end is still to come" (Matt. 24:6, NEB)—these tragedies do not show when or how the world is to end. Jesus warns his disciples against all speculations about God's final action in ending history. "But of that day or that hour no one knows, not even the angels in heaven, nor the Son, but only the Father." (Mark 13:32)

Jesus' concern with the tragedies of human life shows us what it means to live amid them with faith. The suffering and chaos of our world, the power of sin and death in our lives may drive us to despair. In the face of the seemingly unending battering of evil and suffering, we are tempted to conclude that God is not able to save.

In desperation, it is easy to turn to false messiahs, to people and causes that promise us salvation from want, suffering, and death. "Then if anyone says to you, 'Look, here is the Messiah,' or 'There he is,' do not believe it. Imposters will come claiming to be messiahs or prophets, and they will produce great signs and wonders to mislead even God's chosen." (Matt. 24:23-24, NEB) This does not just refer to false religious teachers; Jesus is speaking also of the political leaders and ideologies that demand from people devotion that is religious in its intensity. As Nazism and other forms of dictatorship have shown, some of the most demonic acts in human history come from those who give themselves to self-appointed messiahs or to causes and nations that they believe can do no wrong. Jesus is warning us against the fanaticism that comes to those who have lost hope.

When we lose hope, we tend to get trapped between despair, which does nothing, and fanaticism, which does the wrong thing. In the face of this gloomy analysis of life, Jesus speaks the word of hope to his disciples. "By standing firm you will win true life for yourselves." (Luke 21:19, NEB) When by faith our lives are grounded in his life, we will be able to "stand firm" against despair and fanaticism. This is the "true life" of the faithful disciple.

Traditionally, this teaching has been called the doctrine of the perserverance of the saints. The trouble with the word "perserverance" is that it seems to imply the kind of joyless, dogged determination of those who always expect the worst and usually find it. But what Jesus was talking about is *true life,* the kind of life that is confident, despite the troubles of this world, that God will triumph. The disciple knows this because through his faith in Jesus Christ he is already starting to share in that triumph. The Holy Spirit gives to the disciples, here and now, what Paul calls a "guarantee" or "down payment" of the good things that are to come in the kingdom (Eph. 1:14). Though sin and death are powerful, faith gives us now a beginning experience of the abundant and eternal life that God will bring in with his kingdom. Hope, then, is the real basis of our lives right now. Hope does not come from guesswork about the future, but from the love, forgiveness, joy, and peace we have through Jesus Christ, for these are not fleeting illusions but down payments on a real future.

"Take Heed, Watch"

People have always been tempted to study the events of their own time to find when the world is coming to an end. During the

Middle Ages, the plagues of the fourteenth century were thought to be signs of the end. Luther claimed the pope was the Anti-Christ and that the end was near. During the First World War, some claimed that the Kaiser was the Anti-Christ; they proved this by numerology that showed that the number of the Kaiser was 666—the sign of the Anti-Christ (Rev. 13:18). More recently, the Children of God predicted that the comet Kahoutek in the winter of 1973–74 heralded the destruction of the United States, and their adherents fled the country.

All of these so-called prophets have had to recalculate the date or make a fresh analysis of what was happening in world history. Yet to this day people are prophesying from the Bible about what the Russians are going to do in the Middle East, how the Common Market nations will react, and how the Israelis will respond. They will even draw you maps of the final battle of history.

Jesus' teachings offer such so-called prophesying no encouragement. Instead, he warned, "Take heed, watch; for you do not know when the time will come." (Mark 13:33) In his parables he underlined this repeatedly. God's coming will be like a householder returning unexpectedly from a journey, or a bridegroom appearing suddenly for the wedding feast. These parables explain what Jesus means when he tells us to watch. Watchfulness is not a kind of dreamy looking to an imagined tomorrow, while letting the things of the present go unattended. In Jesus' parables, the servants must be busily at work (Mark 13:34-37), while Matthew 25 says that talents are to be invested wisely and the needy are to be ministered to. We will only be ready for the coming kingdom if we are doing the deeds of the kingdom now. Being ready for what God will do in the future means living in obedient faith now.

This word "watch" has a still deeper significance. If we were building the kingdom of God ourselves, we would not need to watch for it; we could see how we were doing and how near was its coming. But the kingdom is God's gift to us. Its coming is the fulfillment of God's will, not that of humans. The revealing of the kingdom of God comes unexpectedly. Our watchfulness is a joyous openness to the future that believes in the unexpected. We are not fatalistically caught by the evil powers of this world; the future belongs to God.

We cannot pry into the secrets of the future. Watchfulness is the attitude to the future that gives us real life in the present.

Marana tha

Christian hope is focused on the coming of Jesus Christ. The earliest Christians prayed for Christ's return with the Aramaic phrase *Marana tha,* "Come, O Lord." Disciples sensed that the new life they experienced then was real but fragmentary. Their communion with the risen Lord was vital, but they knew that there was a richer, fuller life to be given them when the kingdom of God came.

We can understand their feeling. We know we are forgiven by Christ, but we keep on sinning. We know he is our peace, yet we are still assailed by anxiety and fear. We know he is our healing and strength, yet sickness and suffering are still part of the human lot. To pray for his coming is to pray for the fulfillment of the new life we have started to enter through faith already.

But this hope is never simply personal. It reaches out finally to embrace all that is. This is seen most powerfully in the closing vision of the revelation. The coming of Christ will establish a new heaven and a new earth (Rev. 21:1—22:5). A new community called "the new Jerusalem" is to be established, in which suffering and death are no more. At the center of this new community is Jesus Christ. We will no longer need churches and schools to teach us about him, for his presence will be immediate. Our communion with him and with one another will be complete. And in this new relationship the world will be transformed.

The coming of the kingdom does not mean the loss of the good we already know, but its fulfillment. Paul talks of the kingdom in terms of getting dressed up. He tells us that we will not be "unclothed." Death will not strip us of the love and joy of life. Instead, we shall be "further clothed, so that what is mortal may be swallowed up by life." (2 Cor. 5:4) The love we have for others, now so limited and imperfect, will extend to everyone. The joys we now glimpse so fleetingly will be deep and full enough to embrace all of life.

Words always fail us when we try to express the reality of something genuinely new, for all we have to use are the old words of our everyday speech. This is what the early Christians did when they talked about the kingdom of God. They talked of a city whose streets were gold and whose walls and foundations were jewels, of heavenly mansions, or of a transformed heavenly sanctuary of the temple. Whenever we try to paint a picture of the utopia of the future, we always end up with an enlarged picture of the present.

But as Reinhold Niebuhr warned, the Christian hope is not grounded in "knowing the furniture of heaven or the temperature of hell." Rather, our hope is focused on knowing him who is the source of hope. When we confess the second coming of Christ, we are saying that he is the Lord of the future. This is another reason why we can call him the Lord for all times. It is his kind of life that God has intended for this world. Our hope is that we will enter into that fulfilled life which was his in the resurrection. An early Christian writer caught beautifully the contrast between the present life of the Christian and its future fulfillment. He wrote, "Beloved, we are God's children now." This is our present status in Christ. Then he goes on, "it does not yet appear what we shall be, but we know that when he appears we shall be like him." (1 John 3:2)

The promise of hope is great, yet discouragement is also real. In less than a century after Jesus' day, people were scoffing at those who talked about hope. "Where is the promise of his coming?" they asked. "For ever since the fathers fell asleep, all things have continued as they were from the beginning of creation." (2 Peter 3:4)

How do we feel, almost twenty centuries later? There is a kind of no-nonsense side to modern life that makes us wary of all utopian schemes and poetic dreams. The argument usually runs something like this: "Beautiful hopes for the future may be all well and good. But let's face facts. There is nothing sure but death and taxes." Our pessimism feeds on the fact that human history is full of shattered hopes and unfulfilled dreams. What makes us certain that the Christian hope for the kingdom of God is not one of these?

Charles Kingsley once put the answer this way, "Jesus Christ promised it. Jesus Christ is a Gentleman, and a gentleman never goes back on his word." Our hope is sealed by Jesus' authority. Jesus simply does not go back on his word.

All this is true, but there is something deeper. The reality of the Christian's hope for the coming of the kingdom of God springs from his new life in Christ granted now. By faith we are starting to share in the kingdom life through fellowship with the risen Lord. In service to others we start to see the new community that knows nothing of color or clan being formed. By working for justice in our time, we begin to know what life in the peaceable kingdom will be.

To speak of the kingdom of God is not to daydream of an imagined time or place. It is to project into eternity the life and joy and peace we have in Christ in the present. Perhaps a story can illustrate best what this outlook on the future can mean for Christian life today.

A Modern Parable of Hope

The difficulties we face in trying to find an authentic hope for the future may be seen in the story of two students. One student was brilliant but was assailed by deep doubts and uncertainties about the future. She was almost overwhelmed by the immensity of the task before her as she looked forward to taking the final examination for her degree. Despite excellent work in the past, she feared that she could never pass. Her teachers encouraged her, as did her friends, but to no avail. She had so completely lost perspective on herself and her work that she seemed unable to make her final preparation. She was a victim of a lack of hope that left her feeling futile and disheartened.

Finally her major professor took her aside and said, "We are not urging you to take your final examination so we can flunk you. We see what you have done in the past. We are confident of what you will do in the future." With hope renewed, the student took the examination and passed it brilliantly.

The situation of another student was quite different. This student had studied only indifferently and barely had slipped by on past examinations. Despite this he had the most grandiose dreams about the glories of his future accomplishments. He dreamed of the brilliance of the academic work he would do some day. He lived in rosy expectation of a high-paying and fascinating job that he judged would be his reward. These dreams were very real to him. But they were based on no solid evidence. He was not living in hope but in an unreal fantasy world. In fact, his fantasies were keeping him from doing the patient day by day work he should have been doing. His examinations only brought him failure.

These two students are a kind of parable of people in search of an authentic hope by which to live. At times, we are tempted to be like the student who had done such shoddy work. We retreat into an unreal world of sheer fantasy. While living there, we fail to do what God wants us to do here and now.

As you read the New Testament you can see the problem this kind of false hope created. Paul found it among the Thessalonian disciples. Some of them felt that the end was so near they had best retire from everyday life to prepare for it. Of course, when meal time came around, they still needed to eat. So they started to "free-load" on their fellow disciples who were still involved in the pursuits of everyday life. At the same time we can imagine them demonstrating a kind of spiritual superiority complex based on the claim that they were ready for the end times, while their brethren were still hard at it in the world of everyday life. Obviously this is not the authentic hope given in Jesus Christ, and Paul dealt with the problem in a very matter-of-fact way. He said, "If any one will not work, let him not eat." (2 Thess. 3:10) This rule quickly separated those who were living out of a fantasy from those who were living by authentic hope.

It is more likely that most of us live like that first student, who was almost overwhelmed by the immensity of the tasks before her. We are almost crushed by the uncertainty of the future that seems so threatening. Like that student, we need to be pointed to the solid work already done. The foundation of our hope is in what God has already done in the life, death, and resurrection of Jesus Christ. We need to be pointed to those times when God has touched and renewed our own lives and those of other disciples all around us. What we need to do is to measure again the grounds of hope we have in Christ and thus to find that this hope is large enough and sure enough to win out over any odds. Then we will be free in an authentic hope to do the tasks at hand. Like the able student, our hope can be built on a fact already known and not on an idle dream.

Hope in the future gives us the freedom to live fully in the present, without illusion but also without cynicism and despair. De-

spair is not a Christian virtue. The Christian's pessimism about the
world comes from his realization of his own poor powers to improve
it. His hope for the world comes from his faith in God's power to
make all things new. Our faith in Jesus Christ allows us to share in
a beginning way in the new world that he is bringing to us. Because
we can know him, we are confident that there is a fuller, deeper
revelation to come in the future.

Perhaps what the disciples of Jesus in the twentieth century
need most to do is to grasp more fully a hope in the future. One of
the best ways to start is in sharing with one another the good things
that God is doing for us now, for these good things are the "first
fruits" of a banquet that is coming.

Epilogue

In the seventh century, Paulinus, the great missionary to the pagan tribes of England, preached before King Edwin and his wise men in the north country of England. The king, however, confronted with the decision of accepting Jesus Christ as Lord, hesitated.

Finally he summoned his advisers. As the king held council with the leading men of his kingdom, one of them stood up and addressed him: "Your majesty, when you sit at table with your lords and vassals, in the winter, when the fire burns warm and bright on the hearth and the storm is howling outside, bringing the snow and the rain, it happens of a sudden that a little bird flies into the hall. It comes in at one door and flies through the other. For the few moments that it is inside the hall, it does not feel the cold, but as soon as it leaves your sight, it returns to the dark of winter. It seems to me that our lives are much the same. We do not know what went before, and we do not know what follows. If the new doctrine can speak to us surely of these things, it is well for us to follow it."

King Edwin became a Christian, and after him his whole realm eventually came under the sway of Jesus Christ, for, in the encounter with Jesus Christ, these people found that the mystery of human life, its origin and its goal, was clarified.

The king's wise man had spoken well in his parable of human life. If there is a light that can illumine the darkness of life or remove the mysteries and fears that surround it, then indeed "it is well for us to follow it." There is such a light. At the heart of the Christian message is the promise to each of us by Jesus Christ, "I am the light of the world. No follower of mine shall wander in the dark; he shall have the light of life." (John 8:1, NEB)

The story of Paulinus and Edwin bears the marks of a perennial Christian concern. What is the source of human life? What hope can we hold to as we pass into that unknown called death? These are concerns of human life to which the Christian message has brought new light and meaning whenever it has been preached. Christ has liberated us from life-hobbling superstition and fear of death.

For even in our most robust moments, we all must admit to the fleeting realization that life is brief and uncertain. It is like the flight of a bird from darkness to darkness. And as humans we need to have the mystery of our beginning and ending made clear if we are to enjoy the life we have to the full.

As we think about this parable, we realize that the ways in which people today search for the meaning and purpose of life are very different from those of Edwin, Paulinus, and their followers. We perhaps would want to redraw the wise man's parable. Our concern is not so much with the darkness out of which we have come and the darkness to which we go. Our concern is with the ways in which darkness has crowded into the brief light we already know.

We can no longer count on the old ways of life to guide us safely past the perils of day by day existence. The social and political order on which men and women long have counted for guidance is wavering and unsure. The structure of the family, even the certainty of our own worth, are no longer surely to be counted on as part of the light. Rather, we find darkness in the midst of life.

The cruel paradox of modern life is that in the age of a technology that supplies artificial light abundantly, our inner darkness grows. Unlike King Edwin's council hall, our homes and churches are not surrounded by darkness, even at night. Instead, they are flooded with electric light. But it is a light that does not dispel the darkness of fear. There is the fear of crime, the fear of drugs, the fear of mental illness, and the fear of fear itself.

Yet, though we ask the question of the meaning of life very differently, the answer remains the same. It is in a person, Jesus of Nazareth, who is the risen Lord. His light is a living light, not fixed in any one time or place. "For it is the God who said, 'Let light shine out in darkness,' who has shone in our hearts to give the light of the knowledge of the glory of God in the face of Christ." (2 Cor. 4:6)

Faith is born when we cease to take things for granted. Like King Edwin, we are ready to listen to Jesus Christ when the old certainties out of which we have lived become uncertain. Faith begins to come in the moment when we start to ask questions about who we are and where we are going. The growing child asks question after question, and for the moment, he or she will be satisfied with the answers of parents, teachers, and friends. But the adult still keeps putting questions: What is the meaning of life? What is the point of this world?

We sometimes hear ourselves asking such questions in an especially quiet moment. Sometimes we ask in the face of a stunning tragedy. At other times, we ask amid the tedium of everyday life. In the words of Edwin's wise man, "If the new doctrine can speak to us surely of these things, it is well for us to follow it."

Perhaps it would be closer to the mark for us to speak not so much of a "new doctrine" as of the "New Lord." Faith is being related to Jesus Christ, the true "Lord for all times." He is for every human situation the Lord, the one who is himself the light of the world.

He is the Lord of all times because he bears the light of God into every part of life and death and makes them new. So we can restate the words of the story, "If the Lord can speak to us surely of these things, it is well for us to follow him." Faith is our act of following him. It gives us the answer to the darkness in a life that is abundant and eternal.

Notes

1. J. B. Phillips, *The Young Church in Action* (New York: The Macmillan Company, 1955), p. xvi.
2. P. Althus, *Die Wahrheit des kirchlichen Osterglaubens,* p. 22, quoted in Wolfhart Pannenberg, *Jesus—God and Man,* tr. by Lewis L. Wilkins and Duane A. Priebe (Philadelphia: Westminster Press, 1968), p. 100.
3. Michael Perry, "Easter: Debate and Faith," *The Expository Times* (March 1974), pp. 165–166.
4. "A New Beginning for Charles Colson," *The Christian Century* (July 3, 1974), p. 691.
5. Karl Barth, *Church Dogmatics,* tr. by G. T. Thomson and Harold Knight (New York: Charles Scribner's Sons, 1956), vol. I, part 2, p. 165.
6. "Interpreters of Our Faith: Sarah M. Grimke," *A.D.* (July 1973), pp. 11, 13.
7. *A.D.* (July 1973), p. 47.
8. Maurice Goguel, *Jesus and the Origins of Christianity* (New York: Harper Torchbooks, 1960), vol. I, p. 71.
9. Eric Berne, *Games People Play* (New York: Grove Press, 1964).